P9-BZZ-411

Everything

I'VE EVER DONE THAT WORKED

Hay House Titles of Related Interest

Books

Aura-Soma: *Healing Through Color, Plant, and Crystal Energy,*
by Irene Dalichow and Mike Booth

Crystal Therapy: *How to Heal and Empower*
Your Life with Crystal Energy,
by Doreen Virtue Ph.D., and Judith Lukomski

Gratitude: A Way of Life, by Louise L. Hay and Friends

GROW—The Modern Woman's Handbook,
by Lynne Franks

Messages from Your Angels, by Doreen Virtue, Ph.D.

Soul Coaching, by Denise Linn

Meditation (book-with-CD), by Brian L. Weiss, M.D.

10 Secrets for Success and Inner Peace,
by Dr. Wayne W. Dyer

Trust Your Vibes, by Sonia Choquette

Zest for Life, by Dawn Breslin

Card Decks

Attitude Is Everything Cards, by Keith Harrell

Empowerment Cards for Inspired Living, by Tavis Smiley

I Can Do It® Cards, by Louise L. Hay

If Life Is a Game, These Are the Rules Cards,
by Chérie Carter-Scott, Ph.D.

Words of Wisdom for Women Who Do Too Much Cards,
by Anne Wilson Schaef

All of the above are available at your local bookstore,
or may be ordered by visiting:
Hay House USA: **www.hayhouse.com**
Hay House Australia: **www.hayhouse.com.au**
Hay House UK: **www.hayhouse.co.uk**
Hay House South Africa: **orders@psdprom.co.za**

Everything
I'VE EVER DONE THAT WORKED

Lesley Garner

HAY HOUSE, INC.

Carlsbad, California

London • Sydney • Johannesburg

Vancouver • Hong Kong

Copyright © 2005 by Lesley Garner

Published and distributed in the United States by: Hay House, Inc., P.O. Box 5100, Carlsbad, CA 92018-5100 • *Phone:* (760) 431-7695 or (800) 654-5126 • *Fax:* (760) 431-6948 or (800) 650-5115 • www.hayhouse.com • *Published and distributed in Australia by:* Hay House Australia Pty. Ltd., 18/36 Ralph St., Alexandria NSW 2015 • *Phone:* 612-9669-4299 • *Fax:* 612-9669-4144 • www.hayhouse.com.au • *Published and distributed in the United Kingdom by:* Hay House UK, Ltd. • Unit 62, Canalot Studios • 222 Kensal Rd., London W10 5BN • *Phone:* 44-20-8962-1230 • *Fax:* 44-20-8962-1239 • www.hayhouse.co.uk • *Published and distributed in the Republic of South Africa by:* Hay House SA (Pty), Ltd., P.O. Box 990, Witkoppen 2068 • *Phone/Fax:* 2711-7012233 • orders@psdprom.co.za • *Distributed in Canada by:* Raincoast • 9050 Shaughnessy St., Vancouver, B.C. V6P 6E5 • *Phone:* (604) 323-7100 • *Fax:* (604) 323-2600

Editorial supervision: Jill Kramer   *Design:* Amy Rose Szalkiewicz

All rights reserved. No part of this book may be reproduced by any mechanical, photographic, or electronic process, or in the form of a phonographic recording; nor may it be stored in a retrieval system, transmitted, or otherwise be copied for public or private use—other than for "fair use" as brief quotations embodied in articles and reviews without prior written permission of the publisher. The intent of the author is only to offer information of a general nature to help you in your quest for emotional and spiritual well-being. In the event you use any of the information in this book for yourself, which is your constitutional right, the author and the publisher assume no responsibility for your actions.

Library of Congress Control Number: 2004103941

ISBN 1-4019-0339-8

08 07 06 05   4 3 2 1
1st printing, January 2005

Printed in the United States of America

For Anita, Detel, Dora, Gay, Gloria, Hildur, Kolbrun, Liza, Ronnie, Sarah, and Unnur, in gratitude for shared experiences in England, Germany, Iceland, and Scotland.

Contents

Introduction

Some people have first-aid kits, others keep recipe books, and still others employ tool kits. I keep a resource book (which you're holding in your hands right now)—and it encompasses everything I've ever done that worked. In moments of confusion, indecision, panic, depression, stress, and plain insomnia, I can pick it up and know that I'll find something in these pages that will dig me out and move me forward.

There are things in here that work in darkness, and things that work in daylight. There are techniques that will help you plan your journey through life, and those that will light the next inch of the path when you've lost your way . . . or even dig you out of that swamp you've fallen into.

This isn't a single-answer approach; it's not a guide to the one true Way. There are hundreds of ways, and I've tried many of them. These are my personal "greatest hits," my tested and recommended shortcuts for getting through life.

I'm not a guru, psychologist, or workshop leader. What I *am* is a journalist, a writer, and someone who has followed many paths out of personal need and curiosity. I've collected what's in these pages from workshops and journeys, professional and private crises, altered states and guided meditations, tribal wisdom and family lore, religious tradition and successful improvisation . . . and from the tried-and-true experiences of friends and teachers. But none of it is secondhand, because everything here has worked for me personally at some point in my life.

My resource book represents a lifetime of searching and finding, and I think it's too good and too useful to keep to myself, so I'd love it if it helps you, too. As a writer, I find it very fulfilling when a reader remarks that what I've written has really helped or enlightened them, and that's my fervent desire as *you* read through these pages.

Now, does this really encompass *everything* I've ever done that worked? Of course not. I don't tell you how to fix an electrical outlet or roast a chicken, although I can do those things, too, and they work. I admit that knowing how to fix an outlet and roast a chicken are also life-enhancing, even lifesaving, skills, but you can find household and cookery tips elsewhere. What I'm interested in here is what you can do that will help you feel peace in the middle of a sleepless night, improve the quality of your relationships, help you decide on and follow a true course of action, rekindle your enthusiasm and passion, give you fresh perspectives and new ideas, and throw you a lifeline in the dark nights of the soul that come to everyone.

We begin coping with whatever life throws at us from the moment we're born, and we deal with it in a way that's partially determined by our inherent makeup, the gifts and characteristics already determined by our genes. One baby may cry and immediately be fed. Another, born into a time of famine or into a different family, may cry and never be fed. But for you, reading this book, life isn't so extreme. You've survived infancy and adolescence. You've made certain choices, and maybe you're beginning to learn that what worked in one situation is a disadvantage in another.

You may have done all the things that worked up to now: You may have gotten an education, secured a good job, and been through many relationships. But you wouldn't have picked up this book if you weren't wondering whether there might be something more, something you've missed, something else that might make you happier and turn up the color and volume of your life . . . and perhaps give it narrative and meaning.

You're not alone. Since the Greeks of the fifth century B.C., if not before, people have applied their minds to considering the meaning of life and their part in it. They've wondered about how to behave in relation to everything that's larger than they are—the gods, the universe, and so on. They've asked what it means to lead a good life.

Of course, our lives are immeasurably different from those of the ancient Greeks, but the fundamental questions and longings remain the same: *How, in a time of danger and chaos,* can an individual find meaning and fulfillment? And how, specifically, can I, with my personality, upbringing, tastes, and talents, find a place in the world that satisfies me and connects me to the people who matter in my life?

So this book is partly philosophy and partly self-help. The ancient Greeks were in the business of self-improvement as they argued about the good life on the hillsides of Athens, but where they differed from us today is that they used the tools of rigorous intellectual debate. They weren't in the business of providing emotional comfort, which is the territory of the personal-growth book.

Self-help books offer a refuge when your friends' patience or experience has run out. Self-help books offer comfort. Self-help books are friends. The danger is that they offer easy formulas and glib answers. They can encourage self-indulgence, sloppy thinking, and clichéd thoughts. I hope I don't do that. I'm not offering answers, only ways in which you might arrive at your own. This is why the emphasis is on what *I've* tried that works. I've kept an open mind, I've been eclectic, and I haven't subscribed to one school of thought. I've tried to reconcile what I was taught through tradition with what I've worked out for myself.

Also, this book is partially a memoir—the more I've written, the more I realize that it's a kind of autobiography. You'll learn something about the life I've led, the places I've lived in and traveled to, the jobs I've done, what upsets me, what moves me, and what thrills me. I'm naturally a reflective and contemplative person, and you might be very physical and active. Nevertheless, I might have had experiences that you could find helpful. The things in this book work for me because of who I am and the way I see the world. I am me, separate from you. But we're both human. If we share 90 percent of our DNA with a mouse, I share a lot more than that with you, although you could be another race, another age, another sex.

Whenever I have a new experience, I wonder how it could be useful, how I could relate it to other people. This is where being a writer comes in. I've been a journalist all my working life, which means that I'm innately curious. I get to meet and question a lot of people, sometimes in extreme situations. I've been in presidential palaces and refugee camps. I've interviewed members of royalty, rape victims, millionaires, illegal immigrants, film stars, artists, politicians, musicians, athletes, small children, and the very old. I've learned from all of them, and I love making the connections, picking up the experiences and information that I can pass on.

Being a journalist also means that I constantly have to justify myself to my peers—highly skeptical, critical people. As one former colleague famously said, his first reaction upon interviewing any politician was to think, *Why is this bastard lying to me?* I'm not that cynical, but I'm trained not to be completely accepting either.

I'm also a daughter, a mother, and a friend. My life, like that of millions of women around the world, has been a constant micro-shifting balance between keeping myself, my employers, and my family happy. I've spent years constantly monitoring this balance and being aware that somewhere at my center is a still, true point at which I'm at rest but not inert. It's a point at which self-belief, energy, vision, enthusiasm, and the capacity for happiness are renewed.

This point, which exists in all of us, is like a wellspring that's constantly under threat from pollution, weeds, and other people's garbage: It may be clogged, poisoned, dried up, and built over; and some people might not even be aware that it exists. *I* wasn't even aware, until I started to write this paragraph, that this was how I saw it. We are our own source, our own wellspring. When I say "everything I've ever done that worked," I mean "everything I've ever done that worked to locate, maintain, and protect my own wellspring."

This is constant, vigilant labor, and sometimes we need help. I've taken myself—my body, my intelligence, my heart, my spirit, and my imagination—into all kinds of byways in search of more understanding and experience. I've taken part in workshops and rituals, retreats and processes. I've read books and undergone therapy. I've traveled, cried, danced, sung, walked, explored, painted, and talked with hundreds of others on the same search. Often I've thought, *If only my friends could see me now!*

If I think I'll learn something that will enlarge my experience of life; balance my body, soul, heart, and mind; and give me more understanding as a writer, more patience as a mother, more loving-kindness as a daughter, more sensitivity and perception as a listener, and more creative energy as a writer . . . and if the people offering the something seem to have integrity, talent, and skill, then I'll do it if the moment is right.

The only path I've never walked in pursuit of opening my doors of perception is that of drugs. I've learned to avoid experiences that give you hangovers or letdowns or that might permanently damage you. Besides, there are many more subtle and less dangerous ways to alter your state of consciousness and your view of the world than taking toxic substances. And some of them are included in this book.

This is a circular book, by the way. You don't have to read it in any order. You can dip in and out as you please. I hope it will be of use and comfort to you, but only *you* know what your needs are. I'd add to everything I've said here that there are times when self-help isn't enough, and this book isn't a substitute for medical, therapeutic, or professional aid if you need it. In emergencies, I recommend that you turn to the following essays: "The Emotional Freedom Technique," "Fleeting Feelings," "Calm Down," "Practice Gratitude," "Write a Letter to God," and "The Magic of 20 Minutes."

All the best to you!

Lesley

1
Be Glad You're Free

The following story happened at a point in my life when I was without a regular job and in a great deal of confusion as to what I should do next. A ten-year professional relationship with a newspaper had come to an end, as these things do, and part of me wasn't at all sorry. I was burnt out. Only that summer I'd been having dinner with an old friend who was also a journalist, and she'd confessed (as we sipped our wine) that she wouldn't care if she never gave another piece of advice ever again, and I nodded and said that I wouldn't care if I ever had another opinion.

But having opinions was what I did for a living, and as the days went by, I began to realize that I'd been doing the same thing for too long to have any fresh ideas at all. I found myself approaching editors and saying that I'd love to write for them, while a tired little voice in my head muttered, "Oh no you wouldn't." I'm sure that ambivalence communicates itself just as powerfully as enthusiasm, and I wasn't surprised when these meetings failed to translate into jobs that I didn't really want anyway. So why was I wasting their time and mine? What else could I do?

One very beautiful morning in March, I got up and followed my usual routine: Make coffee. Scan the papers. Make notes of topics I could write about. Call a couple of editors with suggestions and then wait for them to get back to me after their morning meetings. It was 10:30, and I knew that nobody would get back to me before noon. *Forget about it,* I thought. *I'm going for a walk.*

I'm lucky enough to live near Richmond Park, an ancient deer forest and nature reserve on the edge of London, where herds of red and fallow deer graze freely; and woodpeckers, owls, and green parakeets perch in ancient trees. In the woodland garden at the heart of the park, I sat on a log and watched small birds building nests in the treetops while white spring clouds flew overhead in the fresh wind.

I acknowledged, *Really, it's not so bad being out of work.* I thought of all my friends and colleagues stuck behind computers in gray, airless offices while I breathed in the fresh scent of grass and watched tiny birds carrying twigs overhead in the budding branches. Lucky me.

But I still needed an answer to my dilemma. What on earth should I be doing? All I knew was that the way I was going about my career wasn't working.

I began to think about a book I'd bought in Paris a month earlier called *An Inquiry into the Existence of Guardian Angels.* I'd bought it because when I'd flipped through the pages, I'd read that the author was a journalist who'd had the extraordinary experience of being inexplicably saved from a sniper's bullet. He quoted other witnesses to acts of miraculous protection and timely guidance, many of them tough old reporters, foreign correspondents who had inexplicably been diverted from disaster, and seasoned old cynics who neverthe-less acknowledged an intervening mystery at some crucial moment in their life. I could relate to them and their expe-riences, and I was intrigued.

The author's argument was that guardian angels *do* exist. "What's more," he said, "you can build a relationship with your guardian angel by creating a dialogue, preferably out loud. You'll find that angels will communicate, and that they often have a strong sense of humor." It was an interesting book, but I hadn't thought about it until it came into my mind on my log in the wood.

There were no other people in sight on that spring morn-ing, and as I idly watched the clouds and the nest-building birds, I found myself talking out loud. "Okay, guardian angel," I said, "if you exist, I'd like to know what on earth I should be doing about my career. Should I be looking for another col-umn? A full-time job? A contract? With whom? Please give me a clue, and I'd like some sort of answer before I get back to the parking lot."

I remained sitting on my log. The birds continued to twitter and build nests. The little clouds still sailed over from the west. Nothing happened. Eventually I got up and started walking again, and I was so absorbed by the signs of spring all around me that I forgot about my request for an angelic message.

Half an hour later I'd turned back toward the parking lot, and I was crossing a wide-open area of grass when something caught my eye by the side of the path ahead. The area where I was walking was deserted, nothing but grasses bending in the wind and little clumps of trees. Nobody else seemed to be out walking, and I hadn't seen another person in the hour I'd been in the park.

What I found, planted in the grass at the edge of the path where no such thing had probably ever been up to that moment or has been since, was a rough wooden stick with a square of brown cardboard stuck on top of it. Written on the piece of cardboard were the misspelled words: "B glad your free."

Be glad you're free. I laughed and laughed. I turned and looked around 360 degrees. Nobody. "Okay," I said out loud. "Thank you. I get it." And I did get it.

Those words changed everything. I was free. Why was I struggling to chain myself up again? When I got home, I got out my calendar and wrote down a daily reminder not to panic, not to do the conventional thing, not to try to walk back the way I'd come. *Be glad you're free.* The price of freedom is insecurity, but security is often an illusion. Each time I'd wobble or get into a panic, I'd remember that I was glad to be free.

Those words and the manner of their delivery stopped me in my tracks. They turned fear and negativity into hope and courage. They stopped me from banging my head against a wall and encouraged me to take a deep breath and look around. With those words in mind, I took advice that made me decide not to do any work that didn't excite me. I went to art school and began to write about art. By the time I found myself being a columnist again, I was renewed. I had a different per-spective to bring to my writing.

I don't know if I had an angelic encounter that day or whether the experience was purely coincidental. It doesn't really matter. The message worked then, it still does, and it's for you, too: *Be glad you're free . . . because you're as free as you* think you are.

2
Getting Started, Every Time

It's Tuesday morning, and I'm already a day late. Why didn't I start on Monday? I'm sitting at the desk in my office, and I'm feeling besieged and overwhelmed. This is the morning I'm determined to get into the daily rhythm of writing this book. This is the day I stop procrastinating.

I'm feeling slightly sick, because I'm surrounded by piles of files and notes, and I feel that if I open my mouth to scream, a flock of papers will fly in and suffocate me. I know that I'm experiencing what millions of people feel at the beginning of a big project: panic.

I've got project paralysis. My thoughts are jeering at me from the branches of my mind like a flock of sassy black crows: *Think you can write a book? <u>Everything I've Ever Done That Worked</u>? Well, nothing's working now. Who are you? Thought it was easy when you had lunch with the publisher, didn't you? Thought it was clever when you wrote lots of headings down on a sheet of paper, didn't you?*

And what makes you so special that you think you can retreat into your own world to do this? You do realize there's no food in the fridge, right? You know that the frame of your office window is rotting and you meant to call the carpenters two weeks ago. You know there's a pile of ironing waiting for you and that's why you can't find your blue blouse?

And if you're so determined to devote yourself to writing this book, why have you let this week's calendar get so full? Check it out. You've got a dentist appointment tomorrow, followed by an editorial board meeting, followed by choir rehearsal. Won't get much writing done then. You've arranged to see your mortgage advisor the day after tomorrow, and she needs an update on your financial situation, which you haven't prepared. You meant to send flowers to that friend who drove you to the hospital last week, and you ought to call your sick parents to see if their medical test results have come through. . . .

Aaaaargh! That's the thing about having a head full of crows—they never shut up. And they have a wonderful vantage point. Your fears and insecurities are laid out below them like so much roadkill. There's only one way to deal with them, only one cure for procrastination, only one answer to the perennial fear of getting started . . . and that is to *take* an action, no matter how small, that will move you toward your goal.

In this case, my goal is a neat pile of manuscript pages on which I've just typed "The End," but these are some of the many tempting actions that won't get me there: Getting up to make a cup of coffee, taking my ruler and pencil and drawing myself a lovely neat timetable, sticking little labels on all my files and giving them names, cutting interesting and possibly relevant articles out of the newspaper, phoning a friend . . .

All these actions could be useful in the right time and place, but that's not now, not here.

The journey of 1,000 miles begins with a single step . . . always . . . without exception. And the step must be in the direction of the goal and not toward the kitchen or the telephone.

To have *written* the book, I must begin, in some small way, to *write* the book.

I tell the crows to come back again in a half hour if they must. It's Tuesday morning. I didn't start writing on Monday morning, and that's that. Too bad. I have this moment, always this moment. I confront my fears in the best way I know how, by naming them: Failure. Ridicule. Inadequacy. Shame. Not being half as clever as I think I am, and everybody knowing it. Not being able to sustain what I start. But I *have* started. The crows have fallen silent. They may be shuffling their feet along the branches, getting ready to croak, but for the moment they have nothing to say. That's what happens when you really begin. Like Indiana Jones stepping out into the chasm, it's only when you really take the first step that the bridge creates itself under your feet.

I must remember, when this happens all over again tomorrow morning, that it's the steps that make the road.

3
Decoro,
Sprezzatura, Grazia

In 1991 I sat in a rehearsal room in Sapporo, Japan, with the extraordinary composer/conductor Leonard Bernstein and had a conversation with him about the relationship between inspiration and hard work. Bernstein was nearing the end of his life and he was very sick, but I'd just watched him electrifying the London Symphony Orchestra during a rehearsal of Sibelius's First Symphony. Now, with a large Scotch in one hand and a forbidden cigarette in the other, he lay exhausted in the corner of a sofa and talked about how he identified with the composers whose music he conducted. If he'd done his preparation thoroughly, he said, he'd absorb the score into his very bones. He could feel that he was composing Beethoven and Mahler anew in the performance. He *became* the music.

I had an idea to swap with Bernstein, one I'd been given by Anthony Rooley, lute player and specialist in early music. I told Bernstein that he was talking about the art of *Sprezzatura,* and once I'd explained it to him, he agreed.

The musicians of the 17th century, Rooley had told me, believed that a great performance had three elements: *Decoro, Sprezzatura,* and *Grazia.*

Decoro is all the preparation and hard work. It's the lonely research, the checking, the rehearsal, the repetition, and the often futile-seeming effort and drudgery that prepare the ground.

Then comes *Sprezzatura*. It's the art of spontaneity, of standing on the hot spot and performing with such invention and freshness that it's as though the work is flowing through you for the first glorious time. It's the experience of being inspired. This is exactly how Bernstein said he felt about the music he conducted.

Sprezzatura is impossible without *Decoro.* Imagine a mountain. *Decoro*—hard work—is probably nine-tenths of the climb. *Sprezzatura* is the peak—it's magnificent, but you don't hang around there for long. And *Grazia*—divine grace—is the blessed light that illuminates the summit. *Grazia* is what touches a performance in which *Decoro* and *Sprezzatura* are in perfect balance.

But this theory applies to far more than musical performance. It's a Theory of Everything. Leonard Bernstein's life, as I wrote when he died three months later, was a perfect illustration of how these three elements can be the essential ingredients of a successful life, as well as of a memorable concert. Bernstein had astonishing talent but worked like a dog. His performances—even his rehearsals—were full of *Sprezzatura,* spontaneous to the point of shock. And many people, millions, can testify to the *Grazia,* the grace that his teaching, composing, and performing brought to their lives.

You don't have to be a genius to use these elements in your life and work. They apply to every kind of human endeavor from taking school exams to throwing a party to running a political campaign. *Decoro* without *Sprezzatura* will not do. It's no more than uninspired plodding. But *Sprezzatura* without *Decoro* can lead to the leap that misses the trapeze, the blazing but unprepared talent destroyed by nerves, the dazzling lawyer tripped up by the unexpected question. No *Grazia* there.

Work and play are both essential to human endeavor, but I know from experience that the work comes first. Anyone who's become deeply involved in a project knows that moment when a brilliant and creative solution suddenly appears after hours, days, or even weeks of labor. Or as Mark Twain said, "The more I work, the luckier I get."

The luck is *Grazia*. You only get it when you know how to work and then play.

4
Meditation

People who have no experience in meditation tend to think that it's a matter of sitting and letting your mind go blank. On the contrary. Meditation is the practice of unswerving concentration. It's an intense mental discipline, and that's what makes it such a valuable tool in the de-cluttering of the mind and the de-stressing of the heart.

Meditation, for those who've embraced it, is as essential to one's functioning as *barre* practice to a ballet dancer or scales to a musician. Without it there's no internalized self-discipline to hold everything else together. It was the Dalai Lama who said, "The more I have to do, the more I meditate." Meditation means replacing useless fretting and random worrying with a thought-free mental space that allows for renewal and change.

The novice meditator has just as much trouble meditating as a baby pianist might have trying to play Beethoven. I'm not as regular or as disciplined a meditator as I might be, so this is what often happens when I sit down to meditate: I close my eyes and focus my attention on the sensation of my breathing. Then I use a simple sequence of phrases I learned in a retreat led by the Zen Buddhist monk Thich Nhat Hanh. Breathing in, I know that I'm breathing in. Breathing out, I know that I'm breathing out. Breathing in, I remember that I didn't finish clearing up the kitchen, which leads me to the fact that we've run out of bread, and before I know it my mind is racing down the street and into the supermarket.

I pull myself up. I focus again on my breath. Breathing in, I'm breathing in. Breathing out, I'm not at home tonight because I'm meeting friends for a drink. I must remember to return that book I borrowed and, gee, would I be better taking the car, which means finding somewhere to park, but then my friend got towed away last time, which means a hefty fine, and . . . I focus on my breath again.

And so it goes. And so goes everyone. Controlling thoughts is like herding cats. Push them out and they come right back through the door, bringing other stray cats with them. That's why we need to meditate.

When my mind is at its most random and overloaded point, a victim of the need to multitask, that's when I need to meditate. When I have a sense of anxiety deep inside, that's when I need to meditate. When I realize that my thoughts— perhaps about another person or a relationship that's in trouble—are obsessive and repetitive, that's when I need to meditate.

To meditate is to return to a state of stillness out of which organization and order can grow. And it can help settle us down on the physical level, too. I know this for a fact, because meditation immediately lowers my blood pressure (I check it myself).

Like all regular practices, meditation can create long-term changes in attitude and behavior. The regular experience of internal stillness and calm creates a recognition and knowledge of the state that can draw you back in times of turmoil.

People who are meditators have a tool that can keep them from acting out their inner turbulence in a way that harms themselves and others. This is why meditation can be so effective when it's taught in prisons and workplaces.

There are many, many ways to meditate. By this I mean ways to attain a state of inner focus and concentration. Musicians, dancers, athletes, craftspeople, children lost in a game— anyone whose work requires concentration—know what it's like to get into a meditative state—and this state can be experienced *anywhere*. For example, the ultimate aim of *mindfulness* meditation is to make each moment of daily life—preparing breakfast, doing the dishes, pulling weeds in the garden— nothing more complex or more difficult than the simple art of doing and thinking about one thing at a time.

If you've never tried meditation, here's a very simple way to begin: First, find a quiet, undisturbed place to sit. Sit upright, then relax your hands loosely on your knees. Close your eyes and become aware of your breathing. Simply concentrate on your breath without attempting to control it. Be aware of the sensation of the incoming breath in your nostrils, in your throat, and in the rise of your ribs and stomach. When the impulse to release the breath occurs naturally, simply practice the same technique in reverse. That's all. Simply observe, without interference, the sensations of your own breathing.

Your breath is there to save you from distractions, which will no doubt occur in your mind. In fact, your mind has an amazing ability to take you anywhere but where you're trying to be. It's incredible how difficult it is to focus on one simple thing, and how easy it is for our own random thoughts to take charge of the space of our mind.

But our thoughts are *not* in charge of our mind. We are. Meditation is the process of discovering, isolating, and strengthening this "we," this "I"—this calm, detached, compassionate observer that need not be swept away in the chaos of our lives. Meditation is the art of building an inner lighthouse to guide us home in the turbulence.

5
The "Nice Letters" File

Sometime ago, when people wrote more letters than they do today, I began to keep the friendliest ones I'd received and put them in a file. I put a label on the cover and wrote the words "Nice Letters." I still have the file, which has grown, and every now and then I add to it—a thank-you letter, an affectionate postcard from a friend, a swiftly scribbled note on the back of an envelope written by a departing tenant telling me how happy he'd been living in my home. . . .

As a journalist with a regular column, I attracted more letters than most, and I was always touched when people bothered to be nice. Into my "Nice Letters" file went congratulatory notes from editors, as well as supportive letters from readers, who sometimes shared personal experiences they thought I'd relate to. One writer even sent me funny poems. I still get a kick out of those folks who bothered to write down and make note of the fact that, at a particular moment, I'd done a good job, written something perceptive or memorable, cheered them up, or gotten something right. These letters are a record of all the good things, the little indicators that I was on the right path.

Of course, a lot of my letters weren't nice at all. Some readers were horrid, not to mention hopping mad. I even had a letter from one particularly unhinged reader threatening me with violence and rape. Those were the times when I really needed to open my "Nice Letters" file to reinforce my self-worth and my belief in the kindness of others.

Nice letters are like a savings bank of testimonials. They're champagne on paper, a reflection of the person I'd like to be and sometimes am. As for the bad stuff, the heart-sinkers, they go straight in the garbage can.

What happens to nice letters in a world of e-mails? I know that there are plenty of people who save memorable e-mails.

If you do so, I suggest that you print them out and file them, because there's nothing like hard copy. And don't stop writing letters. No e-mail has the force, the element of surprise, and the durability of a handwritten letter in a nice envelope.

This isn't about being vain. It's about bottling encouragement and reminding yourself that if you've gotten it right before, you can get it right again.

Observe Your Passion

6

"It's easy for you," my friends used to say. "You have a talent." What they meant was that they didn't know what to do with their lives. There was no obvious career path, no burning desire, no vision leading them on or energizing them.

Yes, I was lucky. I always knew that I wanted to write, and I *did* have a talent for it, but having a talent doesn't necessarily mean that you know how to use it. A talent is nothing without passion, and I've come to think that when it comes to knowing what you want to do with your life, passion is the best guide of all. Skill can follow.

I started to write this piece because I was thinking of my daughter. I once watched her radiating animation and enthusiasm as she talked about all the things she'd found exciting that week. When she was done talking, she deflated, lowered her head, and said sorrowfully, "I don't know what to do with my life." I told her to listen to herself. She *did* know. Every fiber of her body knew. All she had to do was listen to her passion. So it's a small cosmic joke that she called me up five minutes ago (and two years after that original conversation), hugely excited, to tell me that a radio station was so impressed with the passion that she and her friends brought to their ideas that they were going to be given their own hour-long slot each week called—ta-da!—*Passions.* On this show, they could interview anyone they liked about what made their heart sing. How great is that?

People who feel at a loss tend to go around asking other people what they should do. I've learned to pay attention to myself. Passion is physical, and it actually affects the body: Is my heart beating faster? Am I talking quickly because my ideas are piling up so fast? Is it difficult to switch off? Do I feel more alive?

These are very powerful clues that this is a subject, an area, or a project that you could put your heart into. It doesn't matter what other people think you ought to do, or what would be sensible to do, or what fits their idea of you. If you can't get enthusiastic about something, you're not going to put your heart into it. Do the research. Get the education. Do the math. But if you want the whole picture, listen to your body.

7
The Magic of 20 Minutes

When people learn that I'm writing a book about every-thing I've ever done that worked, they're puzzled and polite. I try to explain that it's not about how to unblock the sink, but more about how to unblock *themselves*. If you were really stuck in a place you didn't like—a bad relationship, an unfulfilling job, a work crisis, a creative impasse—and something in this book got you unstuck and flowing, I'd call that a success.

When people hear this, they get a bit quiet. Then they might ask, "Do you have anything about being blocked?" or "Do you have any advice on how to awaken creativity?" or "My biggest problem is focus," or "I'm so overloaded that I could cry at any minute."

To all of them I'd say, "Yes, I know a trick or two that can help. Try writing a letter to God, try the Emotional Freedom Technique [see page 49], try expressing gratitude even when you're feeling overwhelmed by fear. Try writing it down. Above all, try pulling back from the situation. Get very, very small. Get as small as 20 minutes."

When I feel stuck, unfocused, or miserable, everything feels huge and insurmountable. The problem I'm blocked about seems way too big to tackle. And this makes me feel that I can't or don't want to do it at all. My resistance is huge, so I'll put it off till tomorrow, or sometime when I feel like it. That's what *procrastination* means, by the way. *Pro cras.* For tomorrow. And we all know when tomorrow comes—never. Which is why the problem doesn't get solved, the focus doesn't get pulled back, and the creative breakthroughs don't happen—ever.

What works is to do the smallest possible thing you can contemplate doing. Can you sit down and write a symphony?

No. Can you write a movement? No. Could you write a few bars, maybe 20 minutes' worth? Could you sit at your piano or your notebook for 20 minutes, undistracted by fear, self-criticism, or other tasks? It's only 20 minutes . . . yes, you could do that. And having done that, you might find that you could manage 5 minutes more. And so on.

Never underestimate the power of inertia. It takes far more energy and fuel for a plane to take off than it does to cruise. Cruising is the easy part. That's why the kind of people who finish projects have many ways to get themselves onto the runway and taxiing off. Some writers finish work in the middle of a sentence so that they can start again the next morning. Some begin by writing their own name over and over until their hand and brain start to write something more interesting.

Above all, you have to stay where you are. Artists go into their studios and stay there, puttering, going through the motions, until something clicks in and ideas begin to work. It might take all day for an original idea to happen, but the action of turning up in the studio or at the desk and staying there lets your unconscious know that you're serious. It's like unblocking a sink, after all. Nothing happens and nothing happens, but you keep trying and then, with a glug and a burp, things start moving. And it's the small things, the increments of 20 minutes, that can bring about the shift.

Journalism taught me that the breakthrough often comes with the one extra phone call you don't feel like making. You're getting nowhere and you want to give up, and then the last question in the interview gives you the additional insight, the one great quote you've been waiting for. Art training taught me that the creative solution or original idea comes when you're tired and working, not when you're planning a project from the outside. Somehow, if you stick with the task, you reach a point where your controlling mind lets go and a fresh connection sparks. It often happens when I tell myself, "I'll just do another 20 minutes."

Whatever it is, you have to focus your attention. Even, let's say, if you're in the biggest emotional mess and you don't know where to turn or how to think, allow yourself to really feel, express, sob, howl, and rage for 20 minutes. If you do, you may find that 20 minutes will take you through to a temporary period of calmness, a small clearing where you can begin to think straight. And after that, another 5, another 20. . . .

It's about leverage. Archimedes said that if he had a place to stand, he could move the world. In a tumultuous, frustrating, intransigent world, 20 minutes is our place to stand.

Your Life As a 8
Spiritual Journey

It was presented to me as a homework assignment before a weeklong workshop: "Write an account of your life as a spiritual journey." I was so taken aback that I put the task to one side. I couldn't imagine how to begin.

I wasn't in the habit of thinking of my life in spiritual terms at all. Biographical, yes. Born here. Lived there. Met this person. Had these relationships. Did that job. I could see my life as a constantly updated résumé. I could list educational qualifications and professional achievements. I could see my life as doctors' notes: had measles, pregnant twice, broke ankle.

I could see my life as a chain of addresses or a series of attachments and relationships. But could I see my life as a spiritual journey? Not without a lot more thought.

Off the top of my head, I could probably acknowledge that my life encompassed many things—personal, geographical, professional, and emotional—with moments of what could possibly be considered spiritual experiences occasionally slotted in. But I'd never thought that these moments might add up to a journey, and that there might be any sense of progress, momentum, or continuity. I'd never imagined that so many elements of my daily life would prove to have a spiritual dimension, which, I realized, was immensely important to me.

The exercise of sitting down and looking at my life as a spiritual journey was a revelation. It made me view everything in a completely new light. It taught me a great deal about the deeper values that underlay everything I did. It explained why there had been periods of my life when I'd felt lost and unhappy even though everything had looked good on the surface. Job—fine.

Money—fine. Family—fine. Expression of spiritual values—not fine at all.

First, my adult life didn't involve a lot of churchgoing, although it had when I was a child. My Welsh grandparents took me to a chapel when I stayed with them, and I went to a Church of England primary school where the vicar came in to give a service in the school hall on Wednesday mornings. Yet none of this made me feel holy. Whatever God was, I experienced it, like the poet Wordsworth, out in the fields, in the woods, by the sea. And there were certain pieces of music that, inexplicably, could make me cry.

As I looked at my life as a spiritual journey, I could see how devoid of spirit much of it was. In particular, I could see why my 20s felt so barren under their busyness—all that partying, all that pushing the career forward, all those experimental relationships . . . but where was the spirit, the moments of quiet and nourishment? I could see how periods of social and professional success were simultaneously spiritual deserts and swamps. No wonder I'd secretly felt lost and bewildered.

And I saw with perfect clarity that my spiritual life was nourished and expressed through three main strands—music, art, and nature. I also saw that a very dark and depressed period in my life coincided with a complete lack of creative expression. Which came first—the lack of creative expression or the lack of contact with my Source?

When the workshop started, all of us participants spent a day taking our individual stories and turning them into visual time lines with the help of collages, paintings, and photographs. Our teacher, Gloria Karpinski, threw more questions at us to help us make sense of our jumbled stories.

"Think of your life as a river," she said. "What kind of waters were you born into? Serene or turbulent? Fast-flowing or swampy? What were the turning points, the significant bends? Where was the true self that's always there, no matter what's going on? Are there significant people who crop up on your spiritual journey? A teacher or even a stranger can be more important to your spiritual journey than a parent or a close friend."

By the end of the workshop, we'd produced 12 completely individual works of art, and we'd all learned a lot about what it took to make us happy and fulfilled. We had a much stronger sense of purpose.

What I learned was that those portions of my life where I felt most cut off from nature and blocked from a connection with great music and art were the places where I felt most adrift. I hadn't realized how important music was to me, but there it was, cropping up in my time line again and again, like a life raft. Somehow these connections affected my whole sense of the meaning of life.

This exercise vividly showed me that it's possible to have all the things society says you must have and yet still feel a profound sense of loss and dislocation. What's so striking about it is that you can see exactly where and why this loss and dislocation occurs.

Meaning and happiness, as scores of saints, artists, and philosophers have said, lie not in wealth, status, and possessions. For you, they may lie in a mainstream religious practice;

for me, they don't. So try writing the story of your life as a spiritual journey and, if you didn't know it before, you'll see where your heart really lies.

9
"To Do" Lists

I was taught how to make lists by Superwoman. I was the scattered girl in my first job as a design assistant to Shirley Conran, a woman who much later became famous as the author of a book that told everyone how to organize their lives. Well, she organized *me* first.

Shirley's life was ruled by lists. She would pin her demands for the day up on the wall for the rest of us to read and do. "Give me six great tips on clutter. I want your six best jokes about weight loss. Give me six unique ideas about bedrooms." She also taught us how to keep the lists tidy by crossing each item off with a little vertical line. That way you could instantly see what hadn't been done, and when you'd crossed everything off on your list, you'd get an unbroken vertical line.

Since then, I've lived my life by "to do" lists. At the start of each year, each week, each day, or simply when I feel overloaded and in need of a fresh start, I write the date at the top of a page and then write down everything I have to do. I usually have two separate columns: one for work and one for personal tasks. Then, if I'm being really organized, I draw up a timetable for the day or the week, calculate how long each task will take, and note it. Things are more likely to get done if I take the time to do this. And the time frame helps enormously. When you see that the phone call you really don't feel like making is only going to take five minutes, there's no excuse for not putting it at the top of your list and getting it over with.

"To do" lists may seem anally retentive and control-freaky if you aren't using them already, but if you follow them religiously, they work brilliantly in reducing that internal sense of clutter and panic and in actually getting things done. And they free up your mind for the really interesting things . . . like planning your summer vacation!

10
Knowing What You Want and Asking for It

Assertiveness training was the very first kind of self-development work I ever did. I didn't wake up one morning and think, *Aha, I must become more assertive*. Instead, it happened this way: I just thought, *I need help*.

I was at a stage in my life where I was at home with two children under three and was in the midst of an uncertain free-lance career. Somehow I felt that I'd lost the plot. I had no clue what to do about this, but deep down I thought there must be some way of getting a perspective on my life or on what I was feeling, so I asked for advice from my old friend Ann, who also had two children, a career as an artist, and who was ten years older and wiser than I was.

Ann didn't know what I needed either, but she did know a psychologist and workshop leader whose endeavors she thought were very worthy. Her name was Anne Dickson, and when I called her up, she was about to start teaching an eight-week course on assertiveness training. So that's how I found myself, for the first time in my life, sitting with a group of strangers being given the behavioral tools to work out what I wanted in life and, more important, how to get it without being aggressive, whiny, manipulative, or self-defeating.

Assertiveness training turned out to be about clarity and honesty, and the day came—much more quickly than I expected—when I put it into practice and it worked.

Anyone who has small children knows how difficult it can be to work at home. I wanted to be my independent working self, I wanted to earn money, and I also wanted to be with my children. My husband thought I'd be much happier if I got out of the house, took a full-time job, and made the whole thing organized and clear cut, but I wasn't ready for that. I felt that I wanted some kind of job that gave me regular work but didn't take all my time, so I set up an interview with a former employer, *The Sunday Times,* to see if they had shift work on the news desk.

As I walked the streets between my house and *The Times'* office, my assertively trained brain began to think about the interview, and this is what I thought: *If you're not careful, you're going to get yourself in deep trouble. The news business has irregular hours. You're going to offer your services and you could end up being at the beck and call of a news desk with no fixed limits, which will make it impossible to plan your time or child care. There's no point going in there and just saying you'd love to work for them, because you wouldn't. You've got to be more clear than that.* And then this new crisp voice came into my head and said, "What you want is to work on the news desk for two days a week. That would be perfect. You'd get enough money, stimulation, and experience, and you'd be able to spend the rest of your time at home."

Half an hour later, I sat in the news editor's office and found myself saying, "What I'd really like is to work on the news desk two days a week."

"Fine," he said, just like that. "When could you start?"

I was astonished, although I didn't show it. That week I was able to bounce into my assertiveness-training class and say, "Guess what? This stuff really works."

That was nearly 20 years ago, and I've found the techniques of assertiveness training useful ever since. Whether you're negotiating a job, navigating a sticky patch in a relationship, or returning shoddy goods to a store, it's a great tool for being honest with yourself and clear with other people.

11
The Emotional Freedom Technique

This technique is best described as emotional acupressure. I don't understand why it works, and to be honest, you feel really silly doing it, but it *does* work. It's the quickest, most accessible tool in the box.

Let me give you an example. I woke up today at three in the morning and, in those few seconds between deep sleep and the piecing together of external sounds and sensations that means wakefulness, I sensed an anxious feeling in my solar plexus. Then I realized why I'd woken up.

There had been an emotional crisis during the day. It hadn't been mine, but that of somebody close to me, a person who'd needed comfort and all the calm and stillness I could muster. When I'd gone to bed, I'd deliberately done what I could to put aside the upsets of the day. I'd been walking and swimming, too, so I was physically tired, and I'd fallen asleep quite quickly. But in the cellular cluster of a human tribe, the pain of one affects everyone. It might not have been my immediate problem, but I knew within five wakeful minutes that unless I did something to regain my peace of mind, I was going to have an anxious and sleepless night.

What could I do? Well, the first thing I did was to take a few drops of the Australian Bush Flower Essence *Dog Rose of the Wild Forces,* which claims to protect people from being overly affected by the turbulence of others. Then, although I didn't really feel like stirring myself awake too much, I thought that I'd try to clear the anxiety by using the Emotional Freedom Technique (EFT).

EFT always works for me. As the man who taught it to me once said, "It's weird, and you feel like an idiot doing it, but it works." It involves tapping the tips of your fingers on certain acupressure points in order to release negative energy. While you do so, you say out loud the feeling you want to get rid of. I learned it while participating in a weight-loss program, but when I looked it up on the Internet, I found that it's had many applications since it was first developed by an American engineer named Gary Craig. EFT practitioners use it for combating every kind of negative state from fear of flying to giving up smoking. You can go to a practitioner if you have a complex problem (find one through the Internet), but you can do the quick version as first aid for yourself.

The brilliance of EFT is its speed and flexibility: It's taught as a two-minute stress technique. You could do it as an emergency remedy in the middle of a stressful day—but preferably locked in the privacy of a restroom—because you wouldn't want anybody to see you!

This is what you do. You identify the negative feeling you want to shift. In my case I felt worried, so I said out loud, "Even though I feel worried, I deeply and completely accept myself."

Repeating these words, I started tapping the outside (or "chopping") edge of my right hand with the three middle fingers of my left hand. I did this at least three times, continuing to say my words aloud.

Then, using the index and middle finger of my right hand, I started tapping acupressure points on my face. And I shortened my ritualistic little sentence to its core, to the feeling I wanted to shift.

"Feeling worried," I repeated, as I continued to tap, "feeling worried, feeling worried," and these are the points I tapped, in order:

1   The inner edge of my right eyebrow, on the bone.

2.   Just above the outer end of my right eyebrow, on the bone.

3. Just on the eye socket bone below
    the center of my right eye.

4. The center of my upper lip just
    below the nose.

5. The center of the crease between
    my chin and lower lip.

6. The outer edge of my right clavicle or
    top rib, just inside the shoulder joint.

7. Just inside my right armpit.

8. Then, still repeating my mantra,
    I moved back to tapping my right
    hand, first the outer edge of the
    thumb, just in line with the nail bed.

9. 10. 11.   Then the same place on my index, middle, and little fingers.

12.   Then the karate chop or outer edge of my hand.

13.   Then back to the point between the joints of the third and little fingers. This is what you do while you're tapping on this point: Without moving your head, you raise your eyes from floor to ceiling and back, from left to right and back, and in a big circle. You hum a few bars of music. You count from one to five. You hum again. Apparently this engages different brain functions. You're then supposed to repeat the process.

Some people suggest that you do a kind of audit on yourself by using something called Subjective Units of Disturbance. I find this to be quite a useful way of assessing a problem anyway. How it works is that you assess your problem on a scale of 0 to 10—10 being really painful, 0 being bliss. When you've completed your rounds, you reassess. Invariably you feel better. If you don't think you feel good enough, you repeat the process.

This is all very cumbersome to write about, but very easy to do. On this particular night, it was all it took to calm myself. Two rounds of tapping. One minute, 30 seconds. I could feel my brain disengage from the problem. I put the light out. When I woke up again, it was 7:30.

12
Make Friends with Money

Money and sex are the two issues we find it hardest to talk about, as they cause the breakup of the most marriages. Which is the bigger taboo? Which is hardly ever taught in schools? Which gives you the bigger jolt of fear on a regular basis? Which are you more likely to lie awake worrying about? Which are you most willing to sweep under the carpet or leave to somebody else to take care of? Which produces the most profound sense of panic and helplessness? You're right—it's not sex. It's money.

It's a good idea to make friends with money. It's going to be your daily concern for most of your life, so it doesn't make sense to ignore it or leave it to other people. Even at the start of your working career, there are ways to budget, manage your debts, organize your savings, and work out how much you need to spend and save. Above all, you need to know how to avoid going into debt.

I'm not going to go into all of this here, because there are plenty of good books about basic money management, and there are excellent financial sections in newspapers aimed at ordinary people with ordinary lives and ordinary incomes. There are agencies that can help you restructure loan repayments, and there are independent financial advisors who can advise you on financial products as well. However, beware of advice from institutions, like banks, which have a vested interest in selling you their own products. Money is their business, and they make it on the loans and products they persuade you to purchase.

Taking charge of your money—knowing where it's coming from, where it's going, and exactly what you're spending and saving—is hugely important for your sense of independence and self-worth. It doesn't matter who you are, how you see yourself, or how unworldly and nonmaterialistic you want to be, you can't get away with ignoring this. I've observed that those people who think they're above and beyond money are usually very reliant on other people's. Don't be like that. It's just not mature, and you'll lose friends over it.

Getting in a tizzy and losing control of your finances can lead to dread, confusion, and despair. Never ignore a financial problem because it will grow in the dark. The sooner you admit to it and communicate with the appropriate people, the easier it is to resolve. Noncommunication drives financial institutions mad, and they'll penalize you even more heavily.

If your money is in a muddle, the only way to start gaining control of it is with a moment of reckoning. Start by honestly keeping an account of everything you spend, day by day. You'll soon see where the money is going. And pore through your bank statements, item by item. You may be one of those people who would rather earn more than spend less, but unless you keep an account of your making and spending, how will you ever know where to begin?

Your relationship with money is one of the most important ones in your life and, as with all relationships, truth is the only foundation for making it work.

And, as a rule of thumb, it's always better to make it than take it.

13

When the Sea Is Rough, Mend Your Sails

Sometimes nothing seems to be working. You're between jobs. You're in a relationship desert. You're trying to get projects off the ground but nobody's returning your calls. You should be training for a marathon, but you've turned your ankle. You've reached the stage where you'd just give up and go with the flow if you could, but there *is* no flow.

Sometimes life is just like that. If, when you look clearly at the situation, you seem to be making the right moves and the world isn't responding, it may be time to take the desperation out of your voice and eyes and respond to the deeper rhythm of events. You may have entered a period of winter. Winter isn't terminal, nor is it death. It's simply time to hibernate, to turn your energy inward and do your growing underground.

Westernized culture doesn't support hibernation. People lead global, 24-hour lives where nothing ever sleeps. Television, radio, news, transportation, light, heat, and the Internet all keep going and going. Nothing switches off anymore, and life is going at full force, or seems to be, so when it goes quiet for us it seems like a violation of the natural order . . . but it isn't.

Outside the industrialized, computerized world, whether you go back in time or sideways into different cultures, people understand the slower rhythms of life much better than we do. "To everything there is a season," says the Bible. Gardeners know it. Fishermen know it. Sailors, farmers, and nomads know it. If you look closely at your own life, you can see it, too. The rhythm changes. Sometimes things flourish, and events pile up. Sometimes life feels as though it's gone into slow motion, or even stopped completely.

I've found that the way to survive the little winters of life is to keep working, but reduce your activity and greatly lower your expectations. At times like these, it's never beneficial to force anything. When the sea is rough, mend your sails. When the ground is frozen, live off your harvest. When you can't take the herds into the pasture, give them hay, stay by the fire, and weave your rugs or mend your tents.

Assuming you're not a fisherman or a nomad, there are plenty of things you can do in times of hibernation. These are times for organizing your possessions, harvesting your resources, evaluating your progress, learning new skills, cultivating friendships, catching up on reading or sleep, caring for your body, going within, and reconnecting with your dreams. There may be lessons to be learned, and now you have the time to learn them. Your maps may need to be redrawn, and now you have the time to redraw them, knowing all the while that the season and the energy will shift.

As spring follows winter, times of inactivity are followed by times where your feet don't touch the ground. A season in the wilderness, which can happen to the most gifted, famous, and celebrated people, can quickly become a call back to the marketplace. And when that call comes, you'll be prepared, because one thing you can do in times of inactivity is to have faith in yourself, your abilities, and your dreams. You keep preparing, so that when the change comes, as it always does, you're ready to respond. And the next time the signs of winter come around, you can recognize and greet them without fear.

14
Be a Music Listener

I was standing on a crowded platform waiting for a train into work, reading a magazine that had come in the morning mail. In it there was an article quoting composer John Cage, and it changed my openness to life in an instant. Somebody had asked Cage what his definition of music was. "Music," he said, "is whatever I hear when I put myself in the frame of mind to be a music listener."

I looked up from my magazine, suddenly enchanted. If music was what you heard when you put yourself in the frame of mind to be a music listener, then this grimly crowded suburban subway station at rush hour must be a source of music.

I put myself in the frame of mind to be a music listener. I picked up the rhythm of an incoming train, a bass line. I layered in the brassy squealing of its brakes. A vocal line came from the amplified announcement overheard. There was the choral counterpoint of a dozen different conversations, the soft percussion of feet shuffling on the platform, the woodwinds of blackbirds in the sycamore trees by the track, the cooing and ruffling of pigeons in the roof beams.

Suddenly, through this simple shift in perception, the day was transformed. The mundane, unpoetic world of the station was now full of magic. Even better, this magic, this limitless source of everyday music, was available to me anywhere, at any time. No matter where I was, I simply had to put myself in the frame of mind to be a music listener.

Later that summer I went on a vacation to Crete. The village I stayed in could only be reached by boat or precipitous mountain paths. Its soundscape was the same as that which would have been heard by the Minoans thousands of years earlier. I heard the gentle folding of the tideless crystal clear water on the stones of the beach, the cooing of wood pigeons in the olive trees, the stereophonic clonking of bells from the necks of goats scattered over the steep mountainside, and twice a day the single chimes and clanks turned into a great ringing as the single goats gathered into a rushing headlong flock pouring down the mountain to be fed by the water's edge.

There were moments on that trip when I deliberately sat down in the shade of an olive tree to be a music listener and found that the waves, goat bells, and birds weren't the half of it. The written notes I took while sitting under that olive tree bring the experience back more clearly than any photograph:

> *The music: jazz guitar, <u>pianissimo</u>, from the bar next door. Clang, clang—the goat bells from the cliff across the water. Splash, swoosh, slip, slap—the sea lapping at the shore. Boat engine, a new note, <u>diminuendo</u>, cuts out. Chopping, hammering, from a restaurant kitchen. Slurp, squelch, the sea. Whistling, chirruping, trilling—a canary in a cage. Metallic hammering. Distant bleat. Very faint goat bell. Clink, fork on plate. Rattle, clatter, clunk, a man walks by carrying a crate of bottles along the shore. Soft clunk, a refridgerator door closes.*

Dog barks. Woodwind of small birdsong in the trees, blackbirds and sparrows. The underlying hum of coolers full of cold drinks and fresh fish.

When you listen this intently, wonderful things happen. Your ear becomes attuned to subtle sounds, the constant, unnoticed accompaniment of your day. Your mind suddenly becomes aware of something even more subtle. I began to understand that the world must be full of sounds we can't hear. All around us, extraordinary things are happening that radiate a silent energy. They must have a sound, but our ears aren't designed to hear it. I've read since that sound engineers working in North Yorkshire recorded 54 separate sounds of water in the waterfalls and rivers on the moors. I've heard a vulcanologist talk about the deep song a volcano sings as it builds up to an eruption.

As the days went past in Crete and I played this game more deeply, I began to keep a parallel page of notes that I headed

"Silent Movie." The Silent Movie of the coast in the evening
went like this:

> I can't hear the sound of the sun setting, the sound of
> the color changing on the hills, the sound of the seaweed grow-
> ing under the clear water, the sound of the little gray fish
> changing direction.
> I can't hear the mountains shifting, the peaks growing
> smaller, the moon rising (although it must make a tremen-
> dous roar). I can't hear the darkness falling, the night thick-
> ening, the shadows creeping across the mountain. I can't hear
> the sound of the gold wine trembling in the glass. I can't hear
> the sound of the sea becoming lighter than the sky or the
> sound of the day's heat escaping from the stone.

Of course, a Greek island is full of magic, but you can be
a music listener anyplace where—and this is a huge irony—
music is not playing. The surest way to dull your ears and kill

this particular source of music, to break this subtle connection between yourself and the song of the turning world, is
to drown it out with amplified sound. If any of those Greek
taverns had been playing loud music, I would have lost the
experience of one of the most magical sounds anywhere: the
beehive hum of human voices rising in one collective village-
sized conversation.

Everyone should try putting themselves in the frame of
mind to be a music listener. It's one way to discover that a
seemingly barren landscape is full of life, that the seemingly
inert is endlessly dynamic, that the mundane is miraculous.

15
Let Others Say No

Have you ever seen a two-year-old throw a tantrum? It's an awesome sight—a small human tornado of rage, protest, and affronted dignity. Two-year-olds don't have tantrums because they're bad people; they do so because they're being confronted with the power of "No!" and everything in them is screaming "No!" right back.

But that external *no* wins in the end by getting right inside the two-year-old and setting up home for life. Growing up is a long process of learning what to do and what not to do, and most of us get it in the end, although we do sometimes see adults throw tantrums because they're not getting their own way. It's a horrid sight and, thank goodness, very rare. Most of us have been socialized well enough to control our own morality and behavior; that is, we know how to keep the lid on ourselves. Tongue-biting is good and wise behavior for a two-year-old, but as we grow older, it has its drawbacks. There are situations where self-censorship not only doesn't serve us, but it positively holds us back. We become too self-controlled for our own good.

I'm talking about ambition, creativity, adventure, self-expression, originality, and breaking the rules. If we've been too thoroughly suppressed, we'll have a whole chorus of inner voices going, "That's no good," "Who do you think you are?" "You can't do that, what will people think?" and "People don't do that, nobody's done that before." Those inner voices stop us from doing bad things, but they can prevent us from doing good things, too. The fact is that nothing worthwhile or interesting gets done in this world until people learn to deafen themselves to some of those controlling voices.

I've got a mantra for this phenomenon: *"Let other people say no."* Ignore all the naysayers inside you, and put your ideas and desires out there. What's the worst that can happen—you'll get rejected or people will think you're an idiot? Well, is that worse than living with a constant chorus of inner rejection? Is it worse than never knowing if your ideas would have worked? Is it worse than not knowing if that girl would have gone out with you or if that new friend would have come to dinner? Let other people say no, because the best that can happen is that they'll say yes.

16
The Beauty of Boredom

Boredom must be worse than pain, because I see people willingly heading toward hurt, but most people would do anything to avoid boredom. People will eat too much, take drugs, get drunk, create all kinds of drama, hurt each other, commit crimes— anything, no matter how self-destructive or antisocial—to alleviate the horrors of boredom.

What's so bad about being bored? Well, I was really bored just the other day, and it truly was painful. I'd agreed to go to a seminar on contemporary art, and one of the speakers, an academic who was presumably being paid for her work, gave the worst lecture I've ever heard. It was stumbling, disorganized, and incoherent. She'd lost her notes, and within five minutes she'd lost her audience, too.

It's interesting to observe a roomful of bored people. Nobody can keep still. Everyone becomes restless and wriggly. They pull their hair and scratch their temples, and even hold their heads up in their hands to stop them from falling off their necks in sheer despair. People began to leave. I couldn't, so I wriggled and doodled and scratched and held my head on with the rest, inwardly screaming for the lecture to end. My life slowed to a near stop.

I thought about all the other things I'd rather be doing. I realized, with perfect clarity, what tasks and activities I'd rather be getting on with. So I want to sing the praises of boredom.

Boredom makes your life last longer. Boredom makes you realize what your priorities are. Boredom makes you know, absolutely, as you didn't before, exactly what you'd rather be doing. And boredom forces you to develop your own inner resources. It's boredom, not necessity, that is often the mother of invention. I can remember Sundays as a child when

I could have turned inside out with boredom, afternoons when I'd read my book, done a puzzle, and didn't know what else to do with myself. There were no computers; there was no television—in those prehistoric circumstances, I had to do what people have always done: become creative.

Next time you're bored, don't run to the store or turn on the television. Just sit with it. At the moment when it becomes intolerable, you might find yourself doing something new.

17
Write a Letter to God

I got this idea from spiritual fitness coach Caroline
Reynolds, who uses it in her workshops. If you don't like the
idea of writing a letter to God, and even less the idea of getting a letter back, think of this as yet another way of tapping
in to your unconscious mind. Caroline says it works just as well
if you write it to your Higher Self.

The technique is very simple. Get a pad of paper, and sit
down and write a letter beginning "Dear God." Then write
down, without thinking about it too much, whatever situation
or problem you'd like help with. Sign it "Yours gratefully, [your
own name]."

Now, without stopping to think, write your own reply back. Here's an example:

Dear [Your Name],

I really think you should forgive John so that you can reestablish your relationship. Then, invite him over for a nice dinner and talk and laugh and just have a good time. Put all your old disputes in the past. [And so on.]

Yours truly,
God

Don't stop to rationalize, consider, or criticize. Just keep your hand moving. You'll know when to stop. The answer comes from a wiser, more far-seeing, more compassionate voice, speaking above the stress and panic of daily life. It will surprise you. What it says is personal to you and can be a valuable, ever-present source of advice and encouragement.

As an experiment, because I haven't used this technique for a while, I just stopped to write a letter to God about a difficult family situation. I was immediately struck by how merely explaining the situation as well as my own feelings about it to a Godlike advisor made me think it through much more clearly and fairly than before. After all, if God doesn't know when you're fudging the issue or being self-justifying, who does? So writing a letter to God in itself encourages the highest level of clarity, understanding, and honesty. As I wrote my letter down, fresh solutions were already coming to mind, but I continued, ignoring them.

When God wrote back, in my own hand (or when I tapped in to my own deeper understanding and intuition), it was in a spirit of compassion and wisdom. All at once I could see the other person's point of view and how the situation had arisen. I could also see what was unchangeable about the problem and how I could behave to avoid getting hurt by it. I even had some fresh and playful ideas about how to introduce a new note—that is, how to get out of the habitual emotional gridlock. God's answer, written uncritically and without pausing to think, gave me a fresh perspective, renewed compassion, and a sense of hope . . . and a reminder that there's a valuable technique here that I should utilize more often.

The advantage of writing a letter to God is that you're taking on the voice of an infinitely wise, all-seeing, all-knowing being with the perspective of eternity. There's a spark of that in all of us, which will illuminate your reply.

18
It's Never Too Late

I met my friend Juliette during a part-time adult-education art course. She was a very beautiful girl, a young housewife at home with small children. Eight years later, we were sitting around the dinner table with one of our fellow students, having a reunion. Since we'd first met, Juliette had gotten a degree in theatrical and film makeup, and she'd headed the makeup department of a television drama series.

Now she was about to apply for a master of fine arts program at a major London art college. She was about to hit 40, but her face was just as luminous and energized as it had been eight years before. "It's never too late," she sang triumphantly. "I'd just like everyone to know that it's never too late."

She was right. It's never too late—not until you're dead. I've just celebrated my friend David's 60th birthday at a party where he told us all that he'd finally met and was sharing his world with the love of his life. My former aunt-in-law remarried at the age of 75. My mother started a new career as a teacher at 50.

Maybe it's too late if you're an insect. . . . My favorite cartoon shows two mayflies. One is saying to the other, "It's half past three; it's too late for us to have children." But we're not mayflies.

Just this morning I tore out the obituary of an artist named William Steig, who became a successful children's author in his 60s and created the monster character Shrek in his 80s. On my bulletin board, there's an article about a happy couple who met and fell in love in their 80s, and another about a painter named Edwina Leapman, who composed and recorded her first CD at the age of 70. I once met a millionaire philanthropist and businessman named Ernest Hall who clasped my hand and told me, "I've 65, and last year I recorded a CD of piano music by Lutoslawski and Bartok with the

Leeds Sinfonia, and I'm only telling you this because if I can do it, anyone can do anything."

I began to see that it was never too late when I was in my 20s. Somehow you expect to leave college with all your learning done forever, but life isn't like that, thank goodness. I learned to ride a horse for the first time as an adult because I wanted to go on a horse-riding vacation in Spain. I learned to sight-read music in my 40s because I wanted to join a big choir. I went to art school and learned animation in my 50s because I wanted to prove to myself that I could. Who knows what I'm going to learn next?

The only things that make it too late are biological and medical. It was too late for Zelda Fitzgerald to be a ballerina in her 40s because you just can't be a ballerina at that age, although there are many kinds of dance that are more generous to older people. A flamenco dancer once told me that you couldn't be good at flamenco until you were in your 50s because you wouldn't have lived enough. Zelda just chose the wrong dance discipline, because it's never too late to dance.

Just don't be so relaxed that you leave your fondest ambition for the last minute. Health *does* make a difference. A former English teacher once gave me a single piece of advice, which was never to put things off, because she'd always planned to travel when she retired, but her arthritis became so bad that she couldn't.

Arthritis and travel apart, it's possible to get a new lease on life at any age, and I can't think of anything more inspiring, encouraging, and optimistic than that.

19

Embrace the Dragon

My habitual approach to nature is to choose a nice spot and lie down on it. There's nothing I like better than to recline on my back in a field of long summer grasses and gaze upward, thinking, *Hello, clouds. Hello, sky.* People who talk about "pitting themselves against nature" or "conquering" it seem to have it all wrong. Can't they see that nature doesn't give a damn? They're just conquering themselves.

Nevertheless, I once spent a week in North Wales rappelling down rock faces and scrambling up icy rivers because I loved someone who loved these things, and I thought that if I could learn to love them, too, we could do them together. What I learned was how to deal with fear—and later, that if you approach the same experience from the opposite angle as your loved one, you're going to have trouble sharing it.

So my plan didn't work as far as the relationship went, but it did teach me about moving through fear. And I had a fantastic time because I was with a group of people who were as interested in discussing the emotions involved in all this as they were in rock climbing and such. (The emotions involved in standing at the top of a high waterfall and being asked to jump? Intense!)

The catchphrase for the week, the rallying cry, was "Embrace the dragon," the dragon being our own personal fear. You notice that they, and I, didn't use the word *conquer*. Embracing the dragon rather than conquering it meant that the fear continued to exist, but we faced and included it rather than suppressing it.

I learned that it's possible to embrace the dragon of fear, act with it, and still be afraid. I learned that very thing by rappelling deep down a dark slate mine as I was spinning freely on the rope, 50 feet above the ground. I had no choice but to let myself down, trembling with fear, and then climb the steel rope ladder back up again, sobbing. I survived, but there was no sense of triumph.

It was different with the waterfall. There I stood, quivering, at the top, with encouraging helpers up to their necks in icy water in the river below shouting, "Come on, Lesley, embrace the dragon!" So in the end, I jumped. I disappeared beneath the icy water. I surfaced. I was wet, cold, intoxicated, and exhilarated. Ever since that day, I'm that person you see going straight into a cold sea without flinching, annoying her friends by shouting, "Come on in, it's lovely!" I now know that if they'd embrace the dragon of a ten-second pain threshold, they'd become addicted to the cold-water high that I now enjoy.

But when I jumped into that waterfall, I learned more than the fact that cold water is only cold water. I learned that most fears are simply imaginings that fence you in.

So leap that fence. Investigate the noise in the night. Sit and contemplate the spider instead of screaming and closing your eyes. Look at the snake in the zoo with the same open-minded wonder you can bring to a flower.

And if that fails, I still know that you can act through and with fear. I remember hanging on that rope in the dark and clambering up the rope ladder, and I know that I can get through a difficult experience if I breathe slowly, and consciously take it one small step at a time.

20
Look, Look Again

I'm looking at a white anemone in a blue-and-white vase on the table in front of me. Something makes me stop taking it for granted, put my pen down, and really give the flower my full attention. It's a white anemone. That's what my mind says. My mind is like a secretary following me around, taking crisp notes. It's like a clever schoolchild with her hand always up in the air, waving excitedly with easy knowledge. But is it telling me the whole truth? Let me really look.

The blossom is bowing slightly before me, gazing down on the tablecloth. Its petals radiate round a thick-tasseled crown of gray stamen. *Gray,* says my mind, shooting up its know-it-all hand. Let me really look. Those little seed heads, clustered on white filaments, aren't really gray at all. Brown? Pale coffee? Actually, I look again, and each one is different. At the top, where they're angled toward the light, I can see that each one is white, off-white, cream, around a tiny stripe of green; while at the bottom, they're a dingy cardboard color: buff, string, the color of a bill-collector's envelope.

And is the flower really white? When I look, I can see that no petal, no stripe of a petal, is the same color. The tissue, the flesh of each petal, is very fine, so that there's a transparency that takes on the color of whatever is near it. There, at the heart, is a faint green blush shining through from the leaf behind. The petal's tip gleams where the light passes through the ultrafine webbing of veins that gives the petal its structure. The flower is an object of breathtaking fragility, its delicate surfaces crumpled into a complex layering of subtle lights and shades. And it's a radiant force of energy, its paper-thin petals shooting out from its densely seeded heart with a driving force. Whatever that force is, it holds each fine, fragile petal in place.

When I pay this much attention to a flower—or to anything else mundane in my view: the subtle gleams of light on a green-glazed dish, the fine weave and shading of a tablecloth, the geography of my own hand—many things happen that are good and helpful.

My habitual thinking mind stops. This is the part of my brain that's continually preoccupied with memory and fantasy, the memory of wrongs done and hurts received, the fantasy of events turning out well or badly.

I'm fed by beauty. And I'm reminded that beauty isn't something you find in museums or shops. Beauty is all around me, even at my kitchen table.

I'm in awe. "In awe" is a great place to be. It changes perspective, alters the brain's chemistry, triggers gratitude, and creates a space for fresh thinking.

There isn't a moment in the day when this kind of revelation isn't freely available. It's something I learned in art class, where I was taught to look. I was taught, especially, to look at the relationship of one thing to another, at the spaces between things. I was taught to observe the relationship of one color to another, and I learned that what the mind calls "blue" is 100 other things when you really look. I was taught to *see*.

All the act of seeing takes is the conscious decision to take our attention away from our own internal monologue and our received knowledge and to focus it on something outside in the world, without labeling and preconceptions, if we can.

The reward of attention is revelation.

21
Gifts of Love

Sometimes you can take something and turn it on its head, and something wonderful comes out of it. Creative people—artists, designers, and composers—know that if you're truly stuck, changing the scale, perspective, and angle of a problem can lead to a whole new source of fresh thinking, an undreamed-of solution. I did this once in my journalistic life, and it worked.

I was one of the feature editors of *The Mail on Sunday,* and it was almost Christmas. Now there are really no surprises when it comes to Christmas issues. They're traditionally crammed with suggestions for presents for him or her, for them, and for the family dog; stocking-stuffer ideas for overindulged teens, luxurious treats for grownups, expensive objects for people who probably gave the last present you bought them to their least favorite aunt—and yes, I know, you can hear the spirit of Scrooge in my voice. But there's something about Christmas as a gigantic shopping opportunity that really gets me down.

So I sat in my little glass cubbyhole of an office and brooded, growing more Scrooge-like by the hour. I could feel my annual resistance to the great stuff-and-spend-fest growing with every minute. *Why do we have all these pages urging people to spend money on things they don't want?* I grumbled to myself. And then, slowly, *Why can't we use these pages to get people to give money instead?*

Wait a minute. How would we do that? Suppose we asked all those people whose merchandise we would normally be featuring to donate the goods as prizes. And then we'd pile it all into a photographic studio with kids and dogs and a Christmas tree—as we might anyway. Only this year it would be different. This year everything in the picture—and a lot more that we couldn't get in—would be a prize of some sort. To enter, our readers would have to call in and pledge money, and it would all go to the National Society for the Prevention of Cruelty to Children.

I learned that there's nothing like the infectious, runaway power of a good idea. Nobody had to be persuaded. The editor loved it. Our advertisers loved it. All the publicists who pledged us prizes loved it. And gradually, everyone in the office loved it.

It began in a corner of our office with the fashion-department employees, who were always brilliant at bringing in the stuff everyone wanted (the latest fashion and beauty must-haves), but soon people I'd never seen before were sticking their heads in my door to tell me that they knew manufacturers who'd agreed to donate a car, or a travel agency that would offer a vacation to Fiji.

The photo shoot was hell. Neither the dog nor the children behaved, but the fund-raising was a wild success. The paper put the campaign all over the front page in the week before Christmas, our staff answered the phones, and we raised over a quarter of a million pounds, which, 20 years ago, was worth a whole lot more than it is today. It was the first newspaper Christmas charity campaign, and the best thing about it was that it inspired other newspapers to do the same.

What I'm trying to say here is that it's possible to turn resistance and grumpiness on their heads and make them into something really good. Without my Scrooge-like sentiments about Christmas and a yearning to do something different, an entire recreation center wouldn't have been built. The question that made the difference was not the one I was first asking—"How can I get out of doing this?"—but the one I asked myself next: "If this has to be done anyway, how can I do it differently and make something good out of it?"

It's a question I often ask myself when I'm offered work I don't particularly want to do. And if it can't be answered, then I definitely think twice about doing it.

22

Find Your Own Rhythm

There are many places in the world that still wake up, work, and sleep to the rhythms of the earth and her seasons. For example, if you travel through Africa or India and you begin your journey before dawn, you see people and their animals stirring awake as the light of the approaching sun catches the first smoke from the cooking fires.

We're designed to do the same—to wake up, work, and sleep according to the universal rhythms around us: being more wakeful and active in summer, hibernating in winter, sleeping in the heat of the day, and rising with the sun. The trouble is, the rhythms of the world that most of us know have gone crazy and have detached themselves completely from the moon and the stars—and so have we.

What I mean is that everything changed for us with the Industrial Revolution, when we began to serve the needs of mechanization. The rhythms that drive us have carried on with relentless speed ever since. The electric lightbulb transformed our ability to work after sundown, in the dark of winter. Air travel hurtled us so efficiently and matter-of-factly to distant places that our world is now largely run by jet-lagged people toughing out the disruptive effects of shuttle diplomacy. Computers, telephones and e-mails rudely break time and travel zones and place us all on permanent alert. People used to complain about working nine to five, but for many people, nine to five would be a blessed release. And underneath all this frantic activity, we're the same old cave dwellers, longing to obey the sun.

I carried out an experiment on myself once that has affected the way I've worked ever since. I decided to break out of the nine-to-five orthodoxy and follow the natural rhythms of my own mind and body. I was able to do this because I had taken time off from writing for newspapers in order to write a book. The driving, relentless rhythm of newspapers was difficult to shake off, but I decided, as an experiment over the course of one week, to wake when I woke, begin work when I felt ready, and stop when I felt tired. For that week, I was on my own in a rented house with nobody else to look after or impose their own rhythms on me.

Within 48 hours, it became perfectly clear how my mind and body liked to operate. I'm not a very early riser, however much I wish I were, but getting the kids to school had been getting me out of bed every day. On my own, I woke up around eight, had breakfast, and was sitting at my desk at nine. I then worked in a state of perfect concentration until I noticed that outside thoughts were beginning to penetrate. This was normally around two o'clock.

Then I stopped. I had a late lunch and went out for a walk or to shop. My great discovery was that I seemed to need to take as many hours off as the hours I'd already worked. An hour's break wasn't enough, but after four or five hours, in the early evening, I felt ready for another session at my desk. It was a very productive week and a very happy one.

Ever since then, I've acknowledged that I get most of my work done in the morning. Of course, as soon as I was back home, other people's schedules interfered. Newspapers put me back on their deadlines. Children needed to be driven here and there and fed. Evening social activities used up the energy I'd been able to save for work.

But I'd gotten very useful information, and now I know this: Conventional working hours are nonsense. Offices pay to have people's bodies sitting there, but their useful, creative, energetic minds are often somewhere else. Ask any free-lancer—they know they get far more done at home.

23
The Seduction of Overload

I look back through my calendar entries to a time when I lived in a permanent state of overload. I was a single parent and seemed to be writing a ridiculous number of articles. Unless I was lying to my own calendar, I was sometimes dashing off two and three a day. I was also singing in a choir and rushing off to rehearsals and concerts.

My emotional life was a mess. I was constantly telling myself and anybody who asked how exhausted I was, and I was longing to sink into some kind of oblivion. I was desperate for time to myself, yet I seemed to feel that I wasn't spending enough time with my children. I constantly felt that it was my job to keep everyone around me happy. What did I think I was doing?

I was in the grip of an addiction, the addiction of overload. And once an overload addict, always an overload addict, just like being an alcoholic.

The thing about overload addiction is that it feels so right. A person who's overloaded will complain about being tired and having no time, but will be triumphant in their inability to do it all. The payoffs for their condition are huge. Life feels so exciting and full. The overloaded person feels alive, needed, wanted, and in demand. Overload clicks right into the rigors of the Protestant work ethic: *Thou shalt not slack.* So, as overloaded individuals stagger from appointment to appointment, they take pride in their stress. It's a badge of honor to have a jam-packed calendar, to juggle work and children, to be exhausted. They may feel the guilt of letting friends and family down, but they don't feel the guilt of being unproductive. Who needs any of the other narcotics life offers when you're running on pure, self-generated adrenaline?

Addiction to adrenaline is like any other: Its highs are followed by lows. My calendars tell me that my frantic cramming in of work, activities, and experiences was punctuated with times when I felt as though I'd been hit with a sledgehammer. The weeks when I filed copy like an automaton on speed were followed by days when the work I was doing was effortless and substandard. The intoxication and exhilaration of my emotional roller coaster was followed by days of tearful depression.

A life of adrenaline and overload is thrilling, even fulfilling, but it's not sustainable. Sooner or later something snaps: dates are broken, deadlines are overshot, and friendships and family relationships are compromised and neglected. Worst of all, the mind and body start to suffer.

The first step to overload recovery is recognition. Nothing happens without that moment of personal clarity when the overloaded person says, "I can't go on like this." This is usually accompanied by feelings of despair and frustration because it's impossible to see how the pattern can be broken. At that point, you're on the roller coaster and it's very hard to get off, although illness always works to free you from it. The mind may be driven, but the body will only put up with so much.

Sometimes people know this and ignore it. I was in the office of a very successful magazine editor who hadn't taken a vacation in ten years. She'd come to hate her job. "The only way I'll get out of here is on a stretcher," she said. I tried to persuade her that it might be better to get away for a while. Luckily, she decided to quit before the breakdown happened, but it was only just in time.

Do you really want to be rescued by a heart attack or a car crash?

A calmer, less adrenaline-fueled life can be built with small increments of time. Take a moment to notice what your life is really like. Take five minutes to book an appointment with a doctor, therapist, or life coach, or meet a friend for coffee. Take 20 minutes to leave the computer and walk around the block, to read and think, or to go to the gym or to a yoga class. Take a weekend away, perhaps even a long vacation.

Relinquishing dependence on adrenaline isn't easy because it's the chemical of danger, after all. It's safe and exciting to experience its intoxication through controlled circumstances like sports or dance. But it's *not* safe to let it run your life.

24
West Cork Time

West Cork does it for me. It's a magical corner of southwest Ireland that's both timeless and in constant motion. Clouds drift perpetually overhead from the vast spaces of the Atlantic. The tide constantly ebbs and flows on almost empty beaches, leaving its rippling signature on the sand. You can sit on cliff tops, rocky promontories, in ancient stone circles, and feel suspended in time, en-*tranced*. Landscape and skyscape are the narcotics that soothe all your worries away.

I once spent two weeks in West Cork, endlessly paddling in clear water and lying on my back, looking at the sailing clouds until I felt that I was hovering in a green sky looking down on the blue. When I returned to the city, I felt wonderfully calm and optimistic until it began to rush in at me in all its panic and urgency.

But this time I had a mantra. "West Cork Time," I'd say to myself, and the urgency would creep back like an ebbing tide. Instantly my eyes would look skyward from a crowded sidewalk and find the clouds that float over cities, too. My heart rate would slow, and my blood pressure would fall. Within myself, I tuned into timelessness, and the pressures of the city sighed and deflated.

Of course, if you live in a city, its insistent rhythms and human conflicts will demand that you respond to them on their terms sooner or later. But West Cork Time never goes away. It's always there as a resource. Maybe for you it's Caribbean Time or Kerala Time or Aegean Time. You know what I mean. It's time that's too big to be measured on clocks . . . and it never runs out.

25
Lead a Double Life

I was in my early 20s when I first realized that people can think you're somewhere when you're not. This was a really useful discovery that I've gone on refining and applying ever since. You too can be your own alter ego and lead a double life of sorts.

I first learned this lesson because I'm not great at late nights. One day I overcame the fear of upsetting my friends and being a boring party pooper, and I simply slipped away from a party earlier than everyone else. And that's when I realized that nobody really takes note. The secret is to register a presence and then rely on the fact that most people are far too busy having their own experience to notice that you're not there having it with them.

I then found that this virtual presence continued to operate even if I went away for a whole year, even if I went off to
another country altogether. I took some time off to live in
Ethiopia, and although I thought it might be a bad idea to be
gone so long because my career would be in jeopardy and I'd
fall out of the loop, what I learned again was that nobody really
notices. When I came back from my trip, it was as though I'd
gone down to the bakery for a loaf of bread. Everyone in my
world had been so busy getting on with their own lives that,
apart from really close friends and family, nobody had actually been that aware of my absence.

The same thing happened to a friend of mine who'd been
living in Ethiopia and went home to Edinburgh. "Haven't
seen you for a while," said the barber, cutting his hair.

"I've been in Ethiopia," said my friend.

"Oh aye," said the barber. "Is that on the number 24 bus
route from Princes Street?"

What I know is that everyone lives on their own planet,
in their own time zone, and they don't pay close attention to

yours. You might find this really depressing, especially if you're under the illusion that you're very important and indispensable; however, I find it really liberating and useful. It means that you can go somewhere and come back, and the world will not have crumbled without you.

The way I see it is that we leave little ghostly selves all over the place. People take their memory of you and slot it into their virtual life. "Has it really been six months?" they ask. "Doesn't time fly?" People sometimes tell me, "You've been really busy lately; I've been seeing your name everywhere," when what they've seen is my name in an old magazine they picked up in the dentist's waiting room.

I know that not everyone leaves their name lying around in print, but risk taking off and see. If you take that sabbatical or do that round-the-world trip, you'll find that your world doesn't come to an end. It will just get bigger, more elastic, and a lot more interesting.

I know a jet-setting conductor who's just decided that the art of living is to do as much as possible without leaving home. In his case, that means fewer tours of Japan and Europe and more time writing music and making recordings. Of course we can't all record music that puts our name out there, but when the world is linked by the Internet, we can send our ghostly self out into the world and allow our real self to dig in the garden.

Whichever way you want to do it, know that you *can* lead more than one life at once.

26
Losing Control

You never know if you're learning something that might actually save your life.

I'd been sent off to write an article on a day's rally for Porsche drivers at a Formula One racetrack. Everyone there except me owned a Porsche (and some a Ferrari as well), so I was lent one, bright red. Top racing drivers took us out to practice slaloms and to cruise the track before anyone was allowed to let their Porsches loose on the world-class racetrack.

Of course I was nervous, but first I went out in the passenger seat with one of Porsche's top drivers to pick up a few tips. It's scary going around a racetrack at high speed, and it didn't help my nerves when the driver in front of us hit a bend too fast, lost control of the car, and spun 180 degrees to end up on a grassy mound facing the oncoming traffic.

"What she did wrong," explained my driver calmly, "was to brake hard when she felt the rear of her car drifting out on the bend. If she'd taken her hands and feet off the controls, the car would have corrected itself."

"Yes, yes," I said, earnestly making a mental note of everything he said.

Then it was my turn. I took off down the track, thinking how fast everything feels when you're so near the ground. I hit a bend, felt the car swerve, and forgot everything I'd been told in an instinctive effort to slow the car down. I braked hard. The very expensive piece of machinery I was driving, which didn't belong to me, went out of my control, spun very fast in a screech of brakes and a cloud of dust and rubber, and ended up on the side of the track facing the wrong direction. Very embarrassed, I restarted the engine and crawled sedately back to the start. That was the end of my driving that day.

Fast-forward ten years. I'm driving along a very crowded freeway in a large Peugeot station wagon that's taking me and four children on a week's vacation, and I routinely pull into the middle lane to pass a very long European truck. As I drive alongside it, there's a huge bang, and suddenly I can't see anything at all out of the windshield. The car is spinning uncontrollably at a very high speed, and the four kids are screaming. Everything is a blur, and I know quite clearly that this is it, this is how I'm going to die. At any second, I expect the shell of metal and glass around us to explode and shatter. The end.

In this very brief moment of thought, I remember the time ten years before when I was spinning out of control in a car. This time I remember that in an extreme situation like this one, there's nothing I can do. I must not attempt to control the car in any way—I must let it right itself if it can. I relax my grip on the wheel and take my feet off the controls and wait, as the spinning and banging continue.

The car doesn't explode. Suddenly I find that I can see through the windshield, and what I can see is the crash barrier at the side of the road coming up rather fast at an angle of 45 degrees. This time I know that I can brake and steer, and all at once I'm pulling up on the hard shoulder, straightening up, slowing down, and stopping. I turn and look at the row of white faces behind me, expecting the side of the car to be bashed in, and dreading the injuries I might see, but thank goodness, everyone's safe.

I was vibrating with amazement and gratitude for days—gratitude for being alive, gratitude for the children being alive. And one thing for which I was—am—hugely grateful for was that I had a piece of experience in my armory, and it had worked.

But that incident, which I'll never forget, taught me more than how to drive my car. It taught me that sometimes the right thing to do in an extreme situation is to stop trying to control it.

When we find ourselves in a crisis situation, it's natural to want to take charge, to do something proactive. Sometimes this works and sometimes it doesn't. Sometimes to do something out of reactive fear and panic makes things worse, so it's better to take a deep breath and ride out the shock waves. If you take your feet off the controls and coast—in a state of alertness—it can be very clear when the right moment to take action will come along.

Doing nothing is very difficult, but sometimes it's the best choice.

27
Curfew Love

Twice in my life I've lived under a curfew, and I've loved it. Once was in Ethiopia, in a year of Marxist revolution. Nobody was allowed out on the roads after dark. Everyone had to stay in their own homes, or whichever home they happened to be in when the curfew fell. Only the army and the police were allowed out on the streets, ready to catch any miscreants who happened to be out after dark.

The same thing happened in Afghanistan, three years later, after the Russian-backed coup of 1978. The cutoff was sunset, and that was the end of going out to see friends, eating dinner in restaurants, rehearsing plays, and going to parties.

I was living in both countries with my husband, a doctor who was working for the Save the Children Fund. Maybe being young, in love, and content with each other's company helped, but today we still feel nostalgic about those nights of forced confinement. We spent them reading our way through the longest novels we could find. We got through all of Dickens and Trollope, and we were saving up the great Russian novelists for our next post . . . and our next revolution.

A curfew is an extreme state enacted in conditions of extreme civil unrest, and it imposes rules at the expense of liberty, but I learned that it has another side. Curfew isn't just a cruel confinement, it's also a liberation from restlessness, and from the dissatisfaction of constantly feeling you could be having more fun somewhere else. It's a liberation from the subtle pressure to do the 101 things you do because you ought to, not necessarily because you want to. It's a liberation from the pressure to stay up late to show you were enjoying yourself, and a passport to the pleasure of conversation and early nights without anyone thinking you're a party pooper.

"Total freedom," said the composer Stravinsky, "is total inhibition."

The removal of all boundaries often leads to inertia and inactivity. I've lived all my working life on deadlines, so much so that I find it hard to complete anything without them. The more restrictive they are, the more reassurance they can paradoxically bring.

A peacefulness descends on people who are restrained—the peacefulness of the wayward teenager who's finally been grounded, the driver whose car has broken down, the calm there used to be on a Sunday when every store was closed and the trains didn't run. Now everything's open, and everyone's in their cars, off to spend money and have fun. Total freedom is total gridlock.

It's much easier if you have curfews, deadlines, and constraints imposed upon you, but you can do it yourself if you want to. Or, if you don't trust yourself to keep your own rules, take a retreat where rules will be imposed upon you. Even grown-ups can bloom and relax when choices are taken away from them and calm order is put in its place.

28
Practice Gratitude

There are two regular practices that can transform your attitude to, and experience of, life. One is gratitude. The other is forgiveness. They are the housekeeping tools of the mind and heart. One can fill you with a sense of the richness of life; the other cleans the dark and destructive corners of resentment, anger, and hurt that accumulate, sometimes on a daily basis. If you're really down, it can be difficult to practice either one, but it's probably easier to switch your focus to gratitude than it is to forgive people who are hurting you.

Gratitude is always a good place to start from in the middle of turmoil. It's like a light that you can carry at will from the good places in your life to the dark ones. It will illuminate them.

Gratitude begins as an instinctive, unfettered, and free-flowing response to the positive moments in life. When we're children, it begins as a sense of awe and love, before we're taught to say thank you. Then we sometimes find ourselves being made to say thank you politely, for things we're not at all grateful for, so the sensation and the state get muddled. But you can find gratitude again. Remember the experience of receiving a spoonful of delicious ice cream, a sip of fine wine, an eyeful of moonlight, the sight of the sea, a tender touch, a helping hand, or the clean embrace of your own bed, whether it contains a teddy bear, a lover, or simply rest at the end of a long and tiring day. Gratitude, unforced, will overwhelm you.

Remember those moments when you're in a beautiful place, in beautiful light, in beautiful weather, and all the goodness of the world seems to be spread unstintingly before you. You know, in every cell of your body, that it's sensational to be alive. Your whole self expands to receive your good fortune.

Think about the times when you can hardly believe your luck. You've met someone wonderful who, miraculously, seems to think you're wonderful, too. Or you find yourself in the heart of a group of friends, sustained by cheerfulness and good humor, and you think how lucky you are to have them. You lose a child in the supermarket and after a heart-stopping minute, you find your precious one again. That's gratitude.

Keep this in mind when you're part of a crowd enjoying an extraordinary experience. Your team is scoring a winning goal. You're watching a magnificent play. At a concert, you're on your feet, moving in time with the music. You'll never forget it. You're so lucky to be here.

Narrow your focus. Remember the time you had a cold and somebody made you a hot drink. Remember when you were stranded and somebody offered you a lift. Remember when the money to pay a debt arrived just in time. Remember the stranger who helped you carry a heavy bag up the stairs. These are simple, everyday things, but they connect you with the flow of the world.

Everyone knows what gratitude is, what the sensation feels like. The trick in the conscious practice of gratitude is to reach into this emotional store and be grateful on purpose.

In moments of stress and depression, it's far easier to follow a damaging practice of ingratitude, resentment, rage, and blame. But these obsessive, negative thoughts switch on the chemicals in our bodies that damage our immune system and lead to states of depression and despair. The focus switches from the simple things we have to the innumerable things we don't have, even though others do. Ironically, the more we have, the more we want. But wise people, from the Buddha to the sociologists who have identified the modern sickness of luxury envy, know that want and desire can never be satisfied. The things we think we want are actually the sources of our unhappiness.

The trick is to identify this pattern of thought and change it as soon as it occurs. Reach into your store at moments of trial and despair, and apply the transformative balm of gratitude to your open wounds.

It seems impossible—after all, you have real problems. Of course you do, but they won't be any easier to solve if you only focus on the damage they're doing to you. Negativity, self-pity, and complaints are addictive, easy, and irresistible. They darken your vision so that hope and goodness are invisible. They also become a habit.

I've found that if I practice gratitude instead, starting with the smallest thing (and nothing is too small), my attitude can be swiftly transformed. I like the practice of Mother Teresa, who treated everything that came to her as a gift. "Excuse me, Mother Teresa," said one of her nuns when they faced a long, weary delay at an airport, "we have the gift of several hours' wait." Advanced practitioners of gratitude can look upon everything that happens to them—sickness, accident, bereavement, poverty—as a gift. They're the people who look back at a disaster and say, "Oddly enough, that was one of the best things that ever happened to me."

If you really want to feel enormous gratitude for your messy, problematic life, try nearly losing it. I've never felt so abundantly, humbly, unstintingly grateful, so in love with my life, as I did immediately after surviving a car crash. If your problems aren't life-threatening, you can change your attitude to them by practicing gratitude for the smallest things. And the moment to do this is when you find yourself feeling the least grateful. Stop right there and say the simple words: *Thank you.*

29
Forgiveness

I'd be a hypocrite if I said that I found forgiveness to be an easy thing to practice all the time. I just know that, along with conscious gratitude, forgiveness is the most important step you can take toward peace of mind and emotional freedom.

Life offers us innumerable opportunities to feel resentment, nurture hurts, replay grievances, simmer with justified anger, and burn with betrayal. These strong emotions can consume us utterly. There have been times in my life when somebody has hurt me, and in my constant replaying of the drama, I've been the wronged one, and they've been anywhere on the villainous scale from incomprehensible to downright cruel. If you think of yourself as a nice person, you simply long for others to repent and see things your way. If you aren't troubled by being nice, you may just want to kill them.

I've learned that the only way to survive with grace is to forgive. Nobody is hurt by your pain and anger but you, and the more you perpetuate the pain within yourself, the more damage is done. Take appropriate action by all means—this isn't about being a passive victim. Make your feelings known, write a letter of complaint, even put the matter in the hands of lawyers if you must, but emotionally let it go. There's no victory if you win your day in court and still feel bitter.

Of course you'll find it hard, even impossible, to do this at first. The shock and hurt of being a victim can last a very long time, even a lifetime, and simply saying words of forgiveness will have no immediate emotional impact on you at all. If there's deep and lasting damage, you may find relief and support in professional therapy. But if you initiate the practice of forgiveness, it has the power of the drip of water that wears away the stone.

A friend of mine taught me an inner ritual of forgiveness. Imagine an altar of light. Then imagine putting the person you need to forgive on the altar. Say, "I forgive X for all sins against me, real or imaginary, in this life or any other." Imagine the person dissolving into the light. Then place yourself on the altar and say, "I forgive myself for all sins against X, whether real or imaginary, in this life or any other."

Or, the words of the Lord's Prayer may be enough for you, if you reawaken their meaning: "Forgive us our trespasses, as we forgive those that trespass against us." Whatever our spiritual tradition, forgiveness is expected of all of us.

We can *practice* forgiveness on a daily basis because we're often injured on a daily basis, even in small ways. When somebody cuts you off in traffic, enrages you over the telephone, or is rude in a store, don't fume or fight back. Instead, visualize the person being surrounded with light, and mentally say, "I forgive you, and I release you." Even imagine blowing them a kiss—lightening this up with humor is a very good idea. Then move on.

Without forgiveness, I can tell you what happens. It's not the unforgiven one who suffers. It's the person who can't forgive who carries the wrong, the hurt, the injury unhealed and constantly reactivated. That person is the one whose mind and body are in danger of being permanently damaged by pain, bitterness, and resentment.

Life is too short to suffer and be held by the past in this way. The practice of forgiveness—even when the wrongdoer continues to do wrong—is the only way to freedom and peace.

30
Write It Down

I write everything down. Shopping lists. "To do" lists. Options. Projects. I couldn't travel anywhere without a notebook, and I couldn't sleep without a diary. I've kept one for so long now that if I go too many days without unloading my thoughts and preoccupations onto its pages, I get an uneasy, muddled feeling in my head. Writing everything down brings me clarity.

I don't write for anyone else; I write for myself. And my diaries make very boring reading. I don't write about world events or formulate great thoughts. I don't jot down the kind of specific details or social observations that would be useful to future historians. Instead, I use a diary to keep a record of my family life and to acknowledge and clarify my feelings. By formalizing my interior world on paper, I gain some kind of control and perspective.

Above all, my diary is a place where I tell the truth to myself and jot it down. Because it's a journal of personal record, it's very useful for dispelling the delusions and regurgitations of my own history. I can look back and see what I really thought, not what I now *think* I thought. This can be humbling.

I recently looked at some old diaries and realized, to my embarrassment, that the same boring things preoccupied me ten years ago that preoccupy me now, and that the same resolutions were constantly made and quickly broken. I still fret about needing to lose weight, work harder, and use my talents to their utmost capacity. I remember feeling simultaneous exasperation and relief at the absurdity of my own behavior as I thumbed through the pages. I then gave myself a vacation from pitiless self-flagellation, and the next New Year, I deliberately didn't make any resolutions. I didn't lose any weight physically, but I did lighten up mentally and emotionally. I found freedom in tolerant self-acceptance.

Once you have the notebook and diary habit, you're building your own reference book, your guide to your own life. It's a record of what you really did and how you really felt. It can be full of useful clues and reminders, a repository of insights and ideas. It's a record of people you met; ambitions you had; and circumstances in which you were excited, happy, bored, or sad. Maybe you can create new happiness from the clues you left yourself. And as for those circumstances where you constantly make yourself miserable, your diary provides the information you need to recognize them and step aside.

Above all, a diary is a way to debrief yourself of a day in your life so that your mind is unloaded and ready for sleep. A friend of mine has a nice prayer for the end of the day. It begins, "I release the fullness of this day . . ." I like that. When I say it, I recognize that even the most forgettable day is actually full of details once you begin to replay it in your head or write it down. Often it's in the act of writing itself that the significance is revealed. Or, you might be so full of the emotion of a memorable day that the act of writing is a way of purging.

You don't have to reread what you've written for it to have value, although doing so at a later date—a year, five years, ten years, and so on—might surprise you. I reread my diary at the end of a year to try to make sense of my own experience. How far have I traveled? What worked and what didn't? What did I start and abandon? What ideas were never developed? What new friendships did I make? What old ones did I nurture? What did I learn that I can carry forward? How can I build a new year on the old one?

Keeping a diary is a habit rather than a discipline. Once it's gripped you, it becomes a necessary part of a self-maintenance program, like brushing your hair or washing your face. Only it isn't your body you're maintaining; you're providing a logbook for your heart and soul.

Live Life on Approval

31

Disapproval is bad for you. It sours your heart and turns the corners of your mouth down. Justified complaining, thoroughly pursued, is one thing; a constant nagging sense of irritation is another. It means that your inner dialogue is persistently gloom-filled: *The subway system is hopeless. That woman is wearing too much makeup. Why can't I get a decent cup of coffee around here? Why do people shout when they're on their cell phones? Look at that litter bug. Get out of my way—you might not be in a hurry, but I am!*

There's a trick I use when I find myself mired in a silent monologue of disapproval: I *approve,* on purpose. That is, I start consciously looking for things to praise. Absolutely anything will do to turn the tide. I'm walking along the street cursing the kids who are blocking the way, the loud radio blaring from a passing car, the high speed of that motorcycle . . . stop, stop! My disapproval only hurts *me*.

Okay, now I'll approve of the bright color they've painted that restaurant. I'll approve of the way that man slowed his car down for me to cross the road. I'll approve of the pink flower that store clerk is wearing in her hair. I'll approve of the way that workman is whistling as he waits for the bus. In fact, the more I look at everything going on here, the more there is to approve of. My heart is lighter, and the set of my mouth has changed.

Approval feels better. It's healthier. And if I want to magnify the good feeling, I've learned that it really works to pass the approval on. One day I sat next to woman on the bus who was wearing a wonderful blue robe and turban. She looked so good that I kept looking at her sideways, and the thought grew on me that I really wanted to compliment her. I'm usually quite a reserved person, but I finally took a risk. In my polite English way, I said, "I hope you don't mind my saying this, but I think you look fabulous."

Her face lit up with an enormous smile. "Why, thank you!" she exclaimed, beaming. So in that moment, *two* people relished the effects of approval.

Approval changes the filter of your day. It lifts your mood, multiplies your appreciation of life, and when you pass it on . . . that's cheerfulness squared.

32
Torture Yourself
(in a good way)

Sometimes it's good to torture yourself. I think I've always known it, but when I was reminded of this by the distinguished conductor Sir Colin Davis, who takes a break from learning orchestral scores by knitting fiendishly complicated sweaters, I wrote it down.

I realize that people are torturing themselves around me all day. The men turning purple and dripping sweat onto the treadmills at the gym are torturing themselves. My mother doing her nightly crossword puzzle is torturing herself. My friend training for a marathon is torturing himself. My neighbor translating (unasked and unpaid) a Spanish novel into English is torturing himself.

I did it to myself when I decided to earn a master's degree at the same time I was working full-time. For two years I banged my head on brick walls to learn new skills and tackle difficult problems of my own doing, and I often wondered why I was making life so impossible for myself. Yet I was quite proud of myself, too. I knew that I'd made a commitment to living, growing, stretching, and challenging myself.

"No pain, no gain" applies to anything that's a stretch. Difficulty is good for us, which is why, when life becomes too soft or too boring, we're programmed to seek out challenges. And a difficulty that's overcome is like a blood transfusion.

I remember acknowledging, as I neared the end of my degree, that now that I'd worked this hard and tortured myself so effectively, nothing would ever be as much of a struggle again.

33

My Head Is a Free Space

I say, "My head is a free space." I imagine a border shutting, dividing the free territory of my mind from the clamoring crowd of refugee thoughts that would like to barge in. Outside the border post are the hordes of critical voices, negative thoughts, and corrosive doubts. They clamor. They shout. They press forward, waving their passports, their claims to residency—after all, they're used to coming and going as they please. But they can't come in now. My head is a free space.

I suddenly feel clear and light. Nothing—no thought, no comment—enters unless I allow it to. I choose to exclude all the illegal immigrants of my mind, all the armies of guilt and fear that undermine my ability to act. As I imagine the free state of my head, I can see the invading thoughts for what they are—a demoralizing army that destroys my happiness, my confidence, and my ability to think clearly and consciously.

The feeling makes me realize that I could choose my thoughts instead of having them choose me. Instead of worrying about that insurance claim, I could choose to plan a summer vacation or replay a joyous family lunch. I could recite a piece of poetry to myself, hum a favorite tune, or recall a special place and walk around it in my imagination. Imagination is salvation.

Yet, because demoralizing thoughts and repetitive ideas are accustomed to occupying my head, and because I'm so used to entertaining them, it's very easy for them to slip past my defenses. Before I know it, I'm invaded again. But each time this happens, I'm aware of it sooner and act more quickly. I recite my mantra and expel them: "My head is a free space."

I really don't want to replay an office argument, rehearse a complaint, or mentally rewrite a letter to someone who's let me down. So out with them. "My head is a free space," I say sharply, and the bad thoughts run for the border.

This is an emergency measure, something effective and simple to do when I realize that I'm being driven by thoughts. But it requires that I notice my own thought processes first. Most of us are so habitual in our thinking—so *unthinking,* in fact—that we don't even notice what it is we're thinking about, let alone realize that we have any choice about what goes on in our own heads.

Try this. Try saying "My head is a free space" at regular intervals, and notice what runs for cover.

34
Fleeting Feelings

In my experience, if you're in the grip of a very intense emotion, it's impossible to think or act rationally. It's better not to even try . . . but then how do you deal with these strong feelings?

Once in my life I experienced paralyzing fear, but I did find a way to counter it. (It was an internal fear, by the way. I wasn't in any immediate physical danger or in a situation where I had to think fast, which was just as well, because I wasn't able to think at all.)

What happened was this: The house I lived in at the time had some major structural problems, and I was involved in a big insurance claim. One morning I took a phone call that left me thinking that everything was going to fall through. The insurance company wasn't going to pay up. The house was going to fall down. I had no money to do the work. My house would be uninhabitable and unsalable, and I'd be broke. The vision of my future that suddenly filled me was terrifying—homeless, in debt, trapped. I was a frozen cliché. I was so paralyzed by sheer survival fear that I could hardly breathe.

It was then, as I stood immobile by my phone, that I remembered an antidote. I'd been reading a book by the Vietnamese Buddhist monk Thich Nhat Hanh, who was writing about the Buddhist approach to emotions as forces that worked though you like a weather system. His recommendation for paralyzing moments like mine was to identify the feeling—fear, no question—and to gently repeat this mantra: "Feelings of fear are passing through me."

I stood there by the phone and took a few deep breaths, then I began. "Feelings of fear," I told myself, "are passing through me. Feelings of fear are passing through me. Feelings of fear are passing through me." I wasn't healed instantly; it took perhaps 10 or 15 minutes of repetition (anguished at first, then slowly calmer), for the words to take effect.

Gradually, a gap formed between the overwhelming feelings and whatever "I" was, an entity that observed and was there before the feelings, and would be there after them. The emotions, overpowering as they were, weren't swallowing me up. I was surviving them. I found myself straightening up and walking away. The moment of emergency had passed. And I knew what to do if it struck again, which it never did in quite the same way.

The mantra gave me a vital sense of distance and control, and it was gentle and rational, much kinder than the impatient voice we too often use, which goes, "Don't be so stupid. Pull yourself together. Stop being a baby." The Buddhist voice acknowledges reality and reminds us that it's fleeting. No emotion lasts forever.

Incidentally, the insurance problem was rectified, and I eventually moved from my home. The day before I did so, I managed something that would negate the inevitable stress and disorder of the move: I left my packing boxes behind for a few hours and went to hear Thich Nhat Hanh talk in person. Like his books, he was the essence of calm and humane wisdom. My move went smoothly, and a difficult phase of my life came to an end.

35

The Beauty Way

I first came across the Beauty Way of the Navajo in a book called *Finding Your Own North Star* by Martha Beck. It has been a constant resource for me ever since. I found that it has the power to transform my experience of the mundane, and to shine the light of magic onto the most prosaic, unappealing surroundings. All of this makes the Beauty Way one of the most extraordinary and powerful tools in my box.

Here's how it works: I'm stuck in heavy traffic on a very dingy road in a semi-industrialized corner of south London. My body is cramped and uncomfortable. My mind is resistant and very resentful. My heart is sinking. So I try reciting the Beauty Way:

There is beauty above me. High white clouds are racing across a deepening evening sky. Their form, motion, and free flow remind me of the westerly winds that are carrying them over the city from the open spaces of the Atlantic Ocean, over the green hills of the West Country. They're beginning to catch the apricot warmth of the sinking sun. They draw my mind eastward, to the English Channel, the darkening fields of Belgium and northern France, and even farther east to the Russian mountains, where our icy east winds come from in winter.

There is beauty before me. The taillights of the van in front glow a rich, fiery red. There's an abstract pattern in the flaking paint and rust. The dying sun is reflected in the tall glass wall of an office building ahead. Suddenly it stops being an ugly concrete block and becomes a stack of magic mirrors. The stalled traffic curves ahead, a serpentine line of smoldering red lights leading to the traffic signals. Red—a rich, luminous ruby. Amber—a warm, glowing orange. Green—an intense turquoise like the inside of an ice cave. Why hadn't I ever noticed before how beautiful traffic lights are? Everyday beauty, casually ignored.

There is beauty to the left of me. A quick glance (I need to concentrate on my driving). The car in the next lane is a shimmering abstract of reflections, a dark gleam of high-gloss paintwork, a slick of mirror and chrome. Why have I never noticed what a complex, subtle, mysterious object a car is?

There is beauty to the right of me. To the right there's the same play of light on colors and reflective surfaces as the traffic streams past. As evening falls, a few headlights begin to shine, starlike, in the flow of metal and glass.

There is beauty below me. It's hard to look down in a car, and I certainly can't do it while I'm driving, but the lights turn red again. I'm fascinated by the folded fabric of my own clothes on my lap, the subtle textures, the little canyons of light and shade in the pleats and creases.

There is beauty behind me. A curving chain of lights is framed in my rearview mirror. The shape of the mirror itself miniaturizes and formalizes the abstraction of lights and tones, geometric shapes and subtle curves.

There is beauty inside me. And there is: My anger and frustration have been transformed by the exercise of looking. What was a source of rage and impatience has become a gift offering fascination, pleasure, and revelation. Of course I'd much rather avoid traffic jams, and I don't want to arrive rushed and stressed at my destination, but my experience has been completely altered. I feel that I've been given the priceless opportunity to be able to see the world as a constant source of magic. I am awake and grateful.

There is beauty all around me.

Yes, there is. Thank you.

36

Seek and Ye Shall Find

Once upon a time I designed a ghost train, a dark ride through the ancient underworld. The project took two years, and when I'd finished it, I'd earned a master's degree in design and illustration. I must have been obeying my own advice to torture myself, because over those two years, I went to hell and back in all kinds of different and imaginative ways. I learned about fairground architecture, animation, Greek mythology, mask making, street theater, theatrical lighting, storyboarding, sound design, narrative structure, and an awful lot about death and what people (ancient and modern) think happens to them when they die.

What I discovered filled an entire project report, and I won't bother you with it. But I learned one big thing: Whatever you look for you'll see. When you have an obsession, a project, an *idée fixe,* the world obligingly rearranges itself to suit you. I spent a lot of time thinking about ghost trains, and the world kindly kept presenting me with . . . ghost trains. My life became one giant coincidence. It wasn't that I had permanent ghost-train antennae on my head, although it was *almost* like that. It was as though I was sporting a great big neon sign announcing: "I'm interested in ghost trains."

Here's one example. In the middle of preparing for my course, I took a break and went for a walk in a nearby park. By the pond was a happy little crowd of elderly gentlemen sailing model boats, and when I got up close, I saw a sign that read "Merton and District Society of Model Engineers." My tutors at art school were always asking me when I was going to start making a model of my ghost train, and I was always trying to change the subject. I didn't have a clue how to make a model. But here were some cheerful old gentlemen who obviously *did* have a clue.

"Do you know anybody," I asked one of them, "who could possibly give me a hand?"

"Strangely enough," one of the men said, "our secretary won a prize last year for his working model of a ghost train." Bingo! And likewise, eureka! The antennae worked again.

Seek and ye shall find. A coincidence is only a question meeting an answer in an unexpected way. There's nothing mystical about it, and the more clear and concise you are in your questions, the more quickly and exactly the world will give you a response.

For example, I met a girl in a restaurant recently who'd decided to buy a used car, and she'd e-mailed 12 people to tell them what she wanted. Four e-mailed her right back to tell her about cars they knew about. All she had to do was choose.

Now be aware that the world will meet your expectations in a negative as well as a positive way. Very gloomy people who expect the worst in life are always satisfied. Their lives are, indeed, disappointing to them, even if they look quite satisfactory to other people. But if you spend time with the Eeyores of this world, you realize that they create life in their own image. Their antennae quiver with the daily proof they need that life is a dark and dangerous business. And what's more, they experience all the unhappiness of waiting for things to go wrong.

Things do go wrong, of course, but I've noticed that cheerful people with high expectations of happiness don't waste much time worrying or grieving after the fact. Much better to have a large flashing neon sign on your head that says: "I'm interested in happiness. Come and get me!"

37
A Darn Good Listening-To

A friend of mine was laughing at a phrase he'd heard in a monastery he'd visited. One of the monks was talking about another: "What that man needs," he said, "is a darn good listening-to."

If there's anything we *all* need, it's a darn good listening-to. The feeling of being truly heard is rare, flattering, calming, reassuring, and completely wonderful. Simple attention defuses hurt and anger, relieves tension, and delivers a strong message that the other person is worthwhile and important. It also offers the space and the ground to resolve difficulties.

But pay attention to the people around you. Is listening going on? Or is there an awful lot of interrupting? Are you aware that most people maintain an impatient silence while someone else is talking because they're only waiting for the right moment to jump in with their own ideas and experiences. Are you aware that the yet-unspoken words, "Yes, but . . ." hover over most listeners' heads—that is, if they're listening at all. They could be, and often are, thinking about something completely different.

The feeling of not being listened to can have explosive results (I once threw a plate at someone who wasn't listening to me). Or it can lead to terrible depressions. Someone who isn't being heard can start to feel that there's no point in speaking at all.

The feeling of being listened to can be just as powerful. Giving someone a good listening-to can heal sickness and change relationships. I learned this when my children were teenagers and I came across a book called *How to Talk So Kids Will Listen & Listen So Kids Will Talk* by Adele Faber and

Elaine Mazlish. It made a real difference in the quality of communication in our home. I was chastened to realize that the barrage of questions I greeted my kids with at the end of a school day sounded like a loaded interrogation, an inquisition. I found that if I kept quiet or babbled about something inconsequential, they'd relax and bring up topics at their own pace.

I learned, and I never stop learning, to bite my tongue. I also came to realize that one secret of successful communication is to simply pay subtle attention so that you notice when important things are being said. This isn't an easy thing to do, especially when all of us are so full of answers and good advice. Yes, it's something I keep learning.

I had a conversation with my daughter the other day. She was anxious to quit her job, and I was more than anxious about how she was going to pay her bills. I was so full of things I wanted to say to her that I was halfway through another useful piece of advice before I realized that what she'd just said was, "Do you want to know what I really want to do with my life?" With a mental screech of the brakes, I managed to shut up in time to say, "Yes, please tell me what you really want to do with your life." And she told me.

Listening to people is much harder when you're dying to get your own point of view across, and harder still when you're angry, hurt, or even distraught. That's why so many situations need mediators. If you need to talk about something difficult and emotional with another person and you don't want to use a therapist or facilitator, it's worth trying to agree on some boundaries while you're both calm. It works if you agree on a set time during which each person can speak, uninterrupted, and say what they need to say. It also works if you allow for a pause, and if each person agrees to repeat back what they think they've heard before they say their piece.

Giving people a darn good listening-to is so important that it's worth consciously practicing your listening skills. Just tell yourself that for the next hour, the next day, you'll listen to everyone you meet without interrupting, advising, or judging. You may learn things you didn't know, and you'll definitely feel less stressed.

38
Integrate or Disintegrate

What if you get what you wish for? Will you live happily ever after? Or will you just create a job vacancy for another wish?

A friend of mine gave me a good nugget of wisdom: Don't lust for more than you can integrate. This doesn't mean that you can't have big dreams and ambitions, just that you should be aware of the line between desire and greed. This is such a good idea. When I heard it, I thought that it was meant for me. I've spent a lifetime with my eyes being bigger than my stomach. The result of this, alas, is that one's stomach ends up being a whole lot bigger than one's eyes.

Lusting after more than you can integrate has a lot of other direct and visible consequences. You might find that you have a closet full of once-irresistible clothes that you hardly ever wear. (Think of Imelda Marcos's shoes.)

Or you might find that you have a compulsion to fill a calendar with dates. It makes you feel loved and wanted, but beware of being the type of person who always cancels at the last minute, or who arrives perpetually late and harried because you're trying to cram in one more undigested experience. When friends begin to feel squeezed into someone's life, they eventually squeeze themselves right out again. A friendship that isn't integrated soon disintegrates.

Perhaps, like me, you have a serious book habit. The painter who had to shift hundreds of books to get to my walls said, "Have you really read all these?" "Oh yes," I replied, exaggerating a bit. What about the piles of books beside my bed? If they were apples, they'd all have a couple of bites taken out of them and lie in a rotting heap. But books don't do that; instead, they just lie there patiently gathering dust until I decide to take another bite from one of them. The rot is in the effect they have on my energy, the way they fill up my space. I think back to when I bought each one . . . that inviting pile of new titles in the bookstore . . . not too expensive . . . educational . . . good for the soul. I was brought up to equate books with virtue, so an impulse buy was easy to jus tify. But back home, they soon went on the pile. And unintegrated books just mean more to dust.

And what about the evening classes that are going to change your life, but which are abandoned on the first cold winter night? The correspondence course half completed. The miraculous beauty creams barely touched in the jar. The exercise bike gathering dust in the spare bedroom. The sailboat that never leaves the slip. The gym membership that's never taken advantage of. (Never forget that Mr. Colman of Colman's Mustard once said he'd made his fortune from the mustard that people left on the sides of their plates.)

Why does this matter? Because it's all a waste—a waste of money and a waste of whatever it is you spent the money on— and because it's the visible evidence of a lack of self-discipline and self-knowledge.

What I did that worked, in terms of curbing the lust for more than I could integrate, was to buy a fairly small armoire and never have more clothes than I could comfortably hang in it. It would be a good idea to do the same with bookcases.

I don't think that I, or most of us who aren't monks or nuns, will ever quite crack this one because we all live in a society where happiness is identified with acquisition. But I've learned to refrain from asking, "Do I want this?" and instead ask, "Do I really, *really* want this? Where am I going to put it? Am I ever going to use it?"

I've learned that what I don't integrate, disintegrates . . . and with it, some of my bank balance, my energy, my sense of order, and my peace of mind.

39
Looking Up

This is very simple: Look *up* more. All sad emotional states express themselves with hunched shoulders, downcast eyes, and closed-in postures. Downheaded is downhearted. Don't be downhearted—look up and be uplifted!

If you look up, you'll expand your world. You'll see clouds, weather, the color of the sky, the stars and planets, the flight of birds, the patterns of branches, and the silver trail of planes. If you look up, you'll notice all the creative, expressive, witty, quirky things that architects, builders, and sculptors do that nobody notices. You'll see gargoyles and flags, the gleaming top of the Chrysler Building, the wisp of cloud that streams from Canary Wharf, and the lights on the Eiffel Tower.

You'll see the sky reflected in a million windows. You'll see sculptures and mottoes and coats of arms, ceiling moldings and classical friezes, angels and cherubs. You'll see kites and balloons and aerial messages, giant cranes and skyscrapers. Lift up your eyes and you'll see hills and horizons, a flock of winter geese, and the first swallows of summer.

And yet everyone trudges along, their eyes on the ground or no higher than the next human being.

Remember, freedom is right overhead!

40

Speak in Tongues

If you want your world to expand gloriously . . , to become rich, exotic, and full of new discovery . . . learn another language.

It s little credit to me that I speak two languages, English and French. I owe it to my teachers at school and to my parents, who arranged for me to spend my vacations with a French family.

Mastering another language isn't simply a matter of memorizing vocabulary, struggling with irregular verbs, and being baffled by sentence structure. It's the discovery of a completely different worldview that shows you better than any theory can that your way of thinking and being is not the only way, nor is it the best.

Even the effort made to learn a few phrases for the sake of a vacation yields rewards—smiles, chance encounters, and goodwill. Taking the trouble to say "Please" and "Thank you" in a foreign language is the minimum courtesy travelers can offer, yet all over the world I hear people from English-speaking countries sticking firmly, loudly, and sometimes arrogantly to their native tongue. *We're* the ones missing out.

With a smattering of a language, the world beyond our borders becomes a joyous game. There's something primally satisfying about unraveling a code of sorts. I once took a two-week fast-track course in Greek and followed it with a two-week holiday in the Pelepponese. I did it because I love Greece and I was fed up with being tongue-tied there. The joy I felt in being able to call the plumber to fix a leaking lavatory and to explain to a car mechanic how my car needed help was equal to deciphering a line of Homer.

One thing about languages: If you don't use them, you lose them. They can only be imprinted in the labyrinth of your brain through repetition. I'm out of practice now, and I wouldn't be able to talk to a Greek plumber anymore, but I can decipher road signs and newspaper headlines. I love hearing Greek parents address their babies as Aristotle and Odysseus. I love knowing that the Greeks invented the language of the heart and mind, nostalgia and philosophy, tragedy and psychology. I love the little window in the mind that opens when you learn that the Greek word for "single" is the same as the word for "free."

The joy of learning another language is that there's rarely a direct translation. Entire realms of philosophy are opened up by learning that whole words and concepts are missing in another national brain.

And worlds *are* open to you. My French has taken me in and out of love with French boys, around the Elysée Palace with Madame Mitterrand, through a Berber village with an old peasant in the High Atlas in Morocco, and into drinking contests with French farmers in the Lot Valley.

Learning a language, just for its own sake, can even take your life in a whole new direction. In her first year at a university, my friend Susie decided to take Farsi classes on a whim, and she got hooked. She changed her degree from anthropology to Farsi and spent six months studying in Iran. She subsequently found temporary volunteer work at a human rights agency.

September 11 happened, and Susie, the only Farsi speaker in the office, found herself dealing directly with people in Afghanistan, where they speak Dari, a close relation of Farsi. A year later she was working in Kabul, an experience that was difficult, but valuable and unforgettable.

I can't promise that if you start taking evening classes in Spanish or Serbo-Croatian that something like this will happen to you. But I do know that learning another language could lead to experiences, pleasures, encounters, and possibilities that you can't even dream of.

41
Running-Away Money

My great-aunt Kate always told her three daughters that they had to have running-away money, especially once they got married. She was way ahead of her time on this, but then she knew something about running-away money herself, since she'd run away from her marriage once or twice in her younger days, even though she kept returning home.

Aunt Kate grew up at a time when it was unusual for women to have their own assets, but she knew that running-away money was leverage. It made all the difference between enduring what life threw at you, particularly an unhappy marriage, and having the means to get out and live life on your own terms. Yet when it comes to attaining a bit of freedom and a degree of control over your own destiny, running-away money is a gender-free zone.

Everyone should have running-away money. I'll give it another name. Everyone should have *savings.* I sing the joys, the liberation, and the comfort and protection of savings, from the glorious pile of coins collected from benign aunts and uncles that I saved in my pink plastic piggy bank, to the savings accounts that have several times given me breathing space between commissions and contracts—and even bought me whole years off and the freedom to travel or just say no.

Running-away money means not having to panic if things go wrong. It means that you can take that course or go on that trip. Running-away money means that you can take a sabbatical or a career break. Running-away money means that you need never be anybody's slave—not in a job, not in a family, and not in a relationship.

It was running-away money that freed me to go and live in Africa for 18 months. It was running-away money that meant—when a life coach wondered if I could afford to stop working and reevaluate for three months—that I *could,* and the feeling of liberation was fantastic. It was running-away money that meant I could go to art school.

Savings are unfashionable, while debt is fashionable. Few things enrage me more than the cynical way in which financial institutions suck people into debt as soon as they're old enough to have a bank account. "You can't afford to pay off your loan? Then we didn't lend you enough. Here, have an even bigger loan." For "loan," read "debt."

Your body can tell the difference. Debts and loans, after the brief initial rush of having some money in your hand, produce a sinking, fearful feeling in the pit of your stomach. They haunt you. But knowing that you have savings somewhere makes you feel light and calm.

How do you get that feeling? I know that many young people are saddled with debts and student loans at the very start of their working lives, but you can still save. Saving is a habit, and savings accumulate. One less double cappuccino here, a walk to work there, a homemade sandwich instead of dinner at the café, a night in with a video rather than a night out at the theater. It adds up. And, unlike taking out loans, saving money regularly adds enormously to your feelings of self-control and self-worth. Even saving small change on a regular basis can help you accumulate enough money for a vacation or a celebration.

The important thing is to get in the habit!

42
Sing and the World Sings with You

This is personal to me, but there's an equivalent for you. I joined a choir and it changed my life. I'll go further: I joined a choir and it *saved* my life.

It happened this way: When I was at school, we had a charismatic music teacher named Dr. Moore Morgan. Twice a year, in the spring and summer, Dr. Morgan somehow galvanized half the school into joining his choir and tackling great music. Mozart's *Requiem*. *The Magic Flute*. Haydn's *The Creation*. Mendelssohn's *Elijah*. Most of us learned it all by ear because we couldn't sight-read, and that was when I first learned what it felt like to be possessed by music.

I left school and was swept away by rock and pop, and I danced a lot but I didn't sing anymore. When my 40s rolled around, I began to feel a longing to sing in a choir again. Through my door came a letter from the music teacher at my children's school. He was thinking of starting a parents' choir, no sight-reading required, everyone welcome. A week later I was there, wrapping my vocal chords around Bach's *Christmas Oratorio* and feeling alive again. Within two years, after regular singing lessons with the same teacher, I could sight-read well enough to audition and be accepted into the London Symphony Chorus.

One of the first concerts I sang in (with the London Symphony Orchestra), was *Candide,* conducted by Leonard Bernstein. As we rehearsed in the Barbican with Bernstein and a glittery cast of star singers, I had a second of sharp awareness—that is, I knew I wasn't in Kansas anymore. My home life and my emotional life at the time were bleak. My marriage was breaking up, and I was at a very low point, but in those rehearsals and performances of *Candide,* another door opened for me and I entered a different world—heightened, imaginative, and glorious. I *really* wasn't in Kansas anymore. My membership in the chorus was a passport to Oz.

In fact, singing anywhere—in the shower, in church, or in a choir—is a huge physical, emotional, and spiritual release, and if you're singing a great classical repertoire, it's an incredible mental challenge, too.

Singing gives expression to feelings. It produces endorphins, shakes tension out of muscles, and cancels repetitive thoughts out of brains. It opens hearts and brings exhilaration—literally, *out-of-breathness.* You have to breathe deeply in order to sing properly.

Singing in a choir is also social. If you work alone, as I do, or in a highly competitive and stressful professional environment, it's a blessed release to become a small cog in a larger machine, a tiny part of a greater whole. You struggle in states of individual difficulty to master the music, but you experience sublime moments when the whole comes together and is united and transcendent.

Or you can experience singing quite differently. You can know the intimacy and tender connection that takes place when you sing a baby to sleep with a simple lullaby. Babies don't give a hoot whether you have a great singing voice or not, but they love the feeling of being rocked in song.

If you don't want to join a choir, you can still experience the joy of communal singing in classes and workshops. I've tried Georgian folk singing, overtone chanting, gospel singing and madrigals, jazz singing and musical theater. There are even classes for people who think they can't sing. At every level, I've seen the transformation and transfiguration that occurs when people who start to sing insecurely and nervously open up and bloom. They've let the music in and have experienced the release that occurs at every level when you become an instrument.

The great gospel singer Mahalia Jackson said that when she traveled around the us, she liked to drop in at a local black church and just sing along with the congregation. She called these places her "filling stations." The London Symphony Chorus is one of my filling stations. There's one for you somewhere.

43
Calm Down

Does anything irritate you more than being told to calm down? It's an instant recipe for high blood pressure and enraged thoughts . . . but that doesn't stop it from being a good idea.

I know one way to calm down that was taught me by a Chinese medical practitioner and *chi gong* teacher. I've forgotten everything else he taught me, but this has stuck, and it's my best relaxation-during-the-day and getting-to-sleep-at-night technique, something I use several times a week.

Begin by sitting down, closing your eyes, and focusing on your breathing. Actually, if you feel like doing this in a public place, you don't even have to close your eyes. Don't try to alter your breathing, but be aware of the subtle movements of your body as you take in air and breathe it out. Consciously relax your jaw, let your teeth part, and let your tongue rest with its tip against the back of your lower teeth. Then, focus your attention on the crown of your head and begin this simple process.

Move your attention downward as you recite the following words to yourself on the in-breath. Breathe out and consciously release any tension on the out-breath.

Mind to top of head: "Top of head, relax."
Mind to temples: "Temples, relax."
Mind to jaw: "Jaw, relax."
Mind to neck: "Neck, relax."
Mind to shoulders: "Shoulders, relax."
Mind to upper arms: "Upper arms, relax."
Mind to elbows: "Elbows, relax."
Mind to forearms: "Forearms, relax."
Mind to hands: "Hands, relax."

Rest for a few moments, remaining consciously aware of your breath. Then take your attention back to the crown of your head and begin the second round:

Mind to top of head: "Top of head, relax."
Mind to face: "Face, relax."
Mind to heart: "Heart, relax."
Mind to stomach: "Stomach, relax."
Mind to thighs: "Thighs, relax."
Mind to knees: "Knees, relax."
Mind to lower legs: "Lower legs, relax."
Mind to ankles: "Ankles, relax."
Mind to feet: "Feet, relax."

Then rest again.
If you want to, repeat the cycle.

You can do this anywhere, anytime. As well as calming you down, it will instantly lower your blood pressure.

44

Thinking Straight and Feeling Good

One day the editor I was working for told me to go see a psychiatrist. It's one of the joys of journalism that when you wake up in the morning you have no idea what the day will bring, but this was more off-the-wall than usual. She didn't think I was crazy, but she wanted me to pretend I was.

What had happened was that the Priory, the private hospital of choice for burnt-out rock stars and addicted celebrities, was opening a branch near the city of London, aiming to target burnt-out bankers and addicted traders. "Book yourself an appointment," said my editor, "and write about what it's like."

It didn't take me more than two minutes to realize that any good psychiatrist was likely to uncover a faking journalist in very short order. If I was going to do this job at all, I was going to have to find a way to be truthful, so I found myself sitting in front of a highly qualified psychiatrist telling him the truth, which was this: that I was a journalist, that the previous year I had suffered a period of clinical depression that had been treated with tranquilizers, and that I'd also seen a therapist. I was no longer seeing the therapist and I'd stopped taking the pills after three months, but the early symptoms of that depression—the disturbed sleep, gloomy thoughts, and a feeling of dread in the pit of my stomach—were beginning to return. I didn't want to take any more medication, so did he have anything else to suggest and, by the way, did he know anything about cognitive behavior therapy because I'd heard it was good?

It turned out that I'd booked an appointment with one of the relatively few psychiatrists in Britain who was also a trained cognitive behavior therapist. In his experience, he said, it was effective and suitable for everything except psychosis.

Cognitive behavior therapy is very practical and, unlike any other form of psychotherapy, it puts the techniques for change directly into the hands of the patient. Its premise is that bad feelings come from illogical thoughts, and that once you can identify your faulty thinking, you can counteract it. This well-tried process of self-analysis and correction would make the bad feelings go away.

Controlled trials have shown cognitive behavior therapy to be as effective as medication for depression, and more longer-lasting. Unlike other forms of psychotherapy, it's relatively quick to take effect. No years lying on the couch remembering how mean your parents were to you—cognitive behavior therapy starts with how you feel and act right this minute.

The nice psychiatrist offered me a few sessions to get started, which I didn't take because he also gave me the name of a book for the general reader: *Feeling Good: The New Mood Therapy* by Dr. David D. Burns, based on the author's years of research at the University of Pennsylvania. I found it in my local bookstore the same day and started doing the exercises in it, and that was all I ever needed.

I know exactly how depressed I was because one of the tools in the book is a series of questions that helps you grade your depression from mild to severe. If you're severely depressed—which, according to the index, means contemplating suicide and having worked out the means to do it—then you need to seek medical help.

I was never that depressed, although I continued to use the book over the next couple of months until I realized I wasn't turning to it anymore. It stays on my shelf as a valuable resource, and I recommend it to other people because, unlike many forms of therapy that often depend a great deal on the intuition, personality, and skill of the therapist, cognitive behavior therapy is extremely practical, structured, and logical—that is, it works. (If you prefer a person to a book, a search on the Internet will find you your nearest cognitive behavior therapist.)

45
Flower Remedies

The first time I ever took a flower remedy was when I was soaking wet and shivering after a very cold day spent falling in and out of a Welsh mountain river. Somebody in the group produced a little brown bottle of something called Rescue Remedy and insisted that we pry open our chattering jaws and take a few drops. I remember liking the name, but I had no idea what it was.

Rescue Remedy is the most popular of all the flower essences. People buy it because it rebalances them in times of stress and shock, whether physical or emotional. If you mention the words "flower remedies" to people in the know, they'll say, "Oh yes, Bach"—that's Edward Bach, the British doctor who first developed his range of remedies, including Rescue Remedy, back in the 1930s. But there are hundreds more flower remedies than that.

Fast-forward about 15 years, and I'm reading about possible legislation that would control and restrict all the available alternative remedies and food supplements in UK stores. As a journalist working on the story, I find myself in the offices of Living Tree Orchid Essences, makers of essences from their own specially grown orchids, but also importers of flower essences from all over the world. Their shop, in an old sawmill in a Surrey wood, reveals a world of remedies. Here are flower essences from Australia, France, Italy, the U.S.——north, east, west and south. Here, it seems, are aids to soothe every psychological state and many physical ones, from a broken heart to an anxious or unfocused mind. And yet, if you were to examine the contents of these little bottles chemically, you'd find nothing but water and the spirit that preserves it.

To make a flower essence, you simply steep the flowers in water or, as they do at Living Tree, just place the flowers *over* the water. The theory is that the energy or vibration of the flower is caught in the water, or mother tincture, which is then further diluted and bottled to be taken as drops in times of need. Magic or snake oil? Only experience tells, and mine is good.

I've experimented widely with flower essences. Some remedies have had no discernible effect, and some I return to again and again because they work so well. Perhaps the most dramatic was an Australian Bush Flower Essence called Sturt Desert Pea. I was looking for something relaxing to take at the end of the day, and I actually picked it by mistake. The next day was no fun at all. I felt very depressed, and each little set-back—a bill in the mail or a missed bus——made me tearful. I felt very sad, and I cried on and off all day, which is something I very rarely do. But the day after that was sunshine after rain. I woke up, bounced out of bed, and found myself singing around the house, all tears gone. Singing is a sure sign that I'm happy. The change was dramatic.

I never travel now without a small selection of remedies, in the same way that I carry toothpaste and shampoo. I take

Five Flower Remedy, Dr. Bach's original staple, or I might take Australian Bush Flower Essence's Emergency Essence on long journeys to even out the exhausting and disorientating effects of travel. And I take whatever essence I'm working with at the time, something to focus my mind, boost my energy, or help instill a calm demeanor.

I've experimented with flower remedies consistently for over a year now, during the course of which my state of mind, my emotional balance, and consequently, the external details of my life have changed considerably. Flower remedies have helped me deal with my own moods and, just as important, with the effects of other people's problems. I've given them to friends and relatives, and they've also found them to be very helpful, although I'm cautious about imposing remedies on others.

If a flower remedy isn't the right one, it simply has no effect, but when it does hit the spot, the effect can be dramatic. When I gave Black-Eyed Susan to a hyperactive, stressed-out person, she became very calm and was able to enjoy staying at home instead of being a social butterfly, always afraid of missing any fun. Red Suva Frangipani helped someone else get through the trauma of a breakup.

As for me, flower remedies have helped me become a calmer, more open, more trusting, relaxed person. They've also made an immediately discernible difference when dealing with difficult situations such as going into the hospital—and I experience them as a friendly presence in my life, one that's both subtle and powerful. They're one of the most useful tools in my "first-aid kit."

46
Crystals

When I first began to explore New Age ideas and practices many years ago, I explored this area as cautiously as
someone meandering across a swamp. For every idea I found
valuable, there seemed to be 100 that were absolutely batty
and could only lead to mind rot and ridicule. I could never
shake the voices in my head that tried to dismiss my tentative
explorations as so much tree-hugging, mantra-chanting,
incense-burning nonsense.

So I created boundaries in my mind beyond which I would
not go—ever. And this is where I "put" crystals. People who
believed in the magical powers of crystals, who planted clus-
ters of quartz around their houses or hung them on chains

around their necks, who stuck crystals in front of their computers or swung them on pendulums, were nutty as a fruitcake. You might as well put your faith in sequined wings and tinsel crowns. "If you see me taking interest in crystals," I told my friends, "you'll know I've finally lost it."

Then one day, years later, I came to a point where I decided that it wasn't rational or reasonable to hold such a blanket prejudice. I decided that it was time to put aside a few hours, a day perhaps, to investigate crystals and their possible benefits. What made me change my mind was my experience with flower remedies. I'd discovered for myself, through direct experience, that something for which there was no currently acceptable scientific explanation actually worked and was valuable, even invaluable. So I might as well go full blast and investigate crystals for myself.

I didn't even know at this stage what crystals were supposed to do or how they were supposed to work. So I did what I suggest you do if you're interested: I went to a crystal shop, a fascinating and beguiling place full of beautiful and extraordinary stones, and I spent a small amount of money buying a few crystals that happened to catch my eye. I also bought a couple of books on the subject (one mystical, one quasi-scientific and informative), and I began to read.

The first thing that really surprised me was that when I followed the advice in the books and simply took a piece of crystal in my hand and meditated with it, relaxing and allowing whatever came into my mind to come up, I had a very strong visual experience that changed with each crystal. I tried this contemplation of the crystal with amethyst, fluorite, labradorite, hematite, clear quartz, and rose quartz, and each one gave me a series of vivid images that were peculiar to that particular stone and communicated something of its character.

I was careful to do this before I read too much in the books so that I wouldn't be influenced by what I read. When I went back to the books, my experience of each stone matched what the collective wisdom about its properties seemed to be.

The next thing I tried, also based on the advice of the information in the books, was putting a crystal under my pillow at night. Again, I tried this with different stones. I've done this so often now that I know two things. One is that when you sleep with a crystal under your pillow, you sleep very deeply and soundly. The other is that you can also have very vivid and complex dreams whose character can change with the stone. A rose-quartz dream is not the same as an amethyst dream. I no longer suffer from insomnia since I started this practice, and I lend stones to friends and family members who might have trouble sleeping.

Whatever they do and however they work, crystals are beautiful, mysterious, and enormously enjoyable objects. They have a powerful allure that can seduce people into a lifelong obsession, whether as a jeweler, geologist, or crystal healer.

The field of crystal knowledge and lore is huge, and it embraces pure science at one end and highly mystical belief at the other. I still think an awful lot of nonsense is associated with crystals, but here's something that works: If you're frantic, stressed, and unable to switch off your brain at night, take a piece of hematite, a deep gray metallic stone, and place it under your pillow. This could very well help you sleep.

47
A New Face, a New You

I don't usually recommend "retail therapy," because it's no more than an expensive Band-Aid. Everyone knows you shouldn't shop for food when you're hungry, and it's better not to shop for clothes when you're miserable. But lipstick—that's different. For not much money, you can get something bright, pretty, sweet-smelling, and ego-boosting—a treat. And it doesn't make you fat.

There's nothing at all frivolous or trivial about this. The more dire the circumstances a woman finds herself in, the more power cosmetics and grooming have to hold her together. During the Balkan wars, the women of Sarajevo did their best to look fabulous under siege. Each time they flew in, female war correspondents loaded their luggage with lip-sticks and shampoos to give to the Bosnian women. Looking good is an easy and immediate way to show people that they can't get you down. It's a beautiful way to rebel.

There are ways for men to do this, too. Putting on a happy face is the theme of the opening scene of one of my favorite movies, the Bob Fosse biopic *All That Jazz*. A hungover Fosse, played by Roy Scheider, hits the bathroom, turns up the bouncy baroque music, pops some pills, splashes in some eye drops, and looks in the mirror while exclaiming: "It's showtime!"

Life *is* showtime. And sometimes you have to make up to fake it. It's a cheap trick, but it's fun and it works.

48
Tribal Mothering

Here's the dilemma. You live in a small community and everybody knows your name. There can be some comfort in this, but no anonymity and no freedom, which is one reason why the world's cities are teeming with people who have come from villages.

So here's another dilemma. You live in a large city, a community that often doesn't feel like a community at all. Nobody knows your name. There's freedom in this, but no support. Where, in all the millions of people around you, are the village elders? The wise women? The young braves to come to your rescue? The tribal mothers?

I never felt this lack of tribal support as acutely as when I was bringing up teenagers as a single parent in the city. I saw how easy and dangerous it would be for my children's heartbeats to tune themselves to urban jungle drums rather than the quieter pulse of their own home. I knew that I needed reinforcement from a bigger group. My own family is typically scattered, separated by many miles. We manage to gather for holidays and birthdays, but there's none of that frequent, casual contact that makes extended families out of nuclear ones and keeps us all bonded into the pattern of each other's daily lives.

One day we had a big family crisis, one that happens to other people and you hope never happens to you. I'd been away for the weekend, leaving my 15-year-old daughter with a friend's family. When I returned home, all my instincts told me that something was wrong. Maybe it was the slightly rearranged furniture. Maybe it was the lights burning everywhere. Maybe it was the muddy footprints on the sofa. Definitely it was the fact that my daughter was somehow at home after all and making the unprecedented claim that she'd been cleaning the house.

Party time. Thanks to neighbors, the truth came out fast. My elder daughter, with the help of a lot of deceit, had returned home with her friends and had invited 120 people, most of them strangers, into my now battered and grubby house. Within minutes, I realized that all her close friends, the little toads, had also lied to their parents about where they'd been and had joined in the vandalism of my home. As soon as my delinquent daughter realized that I was serious about calling each family in turn, she sheepishly handed over her address book.

It was tribal-mothering time. One by one, I asked each of those parents to turn up at my home the next day with their daughters and hash the whole thing out. One by one they arrived, embarrassed child in tow, and we sat in a big circle and began to say what we felt about what had happened. I talked. The mothers talked. The daughters got their chance to talk. We decided on appropriate punishments. We cleared the air. We ended up with reminiscences and laughter. We made friends. We knew that, in the maelstrom of parenting teenagers, we weren't alone.

This was a huge help and comfort over the next few years. The parents knew they had support at the end of a phone line. The girls knew that there were rules. It wasn't a matter of deceiving one parent anymore. They knew we would communicate. And, ten years later, those girls are still good friends—and now responsible, hardworking adults with their delinquent years behind them.

You don't have to be a single parent to find the concept of the tribe a huge comfort. A group that's going through the same life experiences as you are can be a lifesaver. At different times in my life, I've found myself part of different groups—made up of colleagues, students, choir members, and artists—that have led to lifelong friendships. Group energy can carry forward a person who would be lagging on their own.

It's different from normal friendships because it has a framework, a purpose. The thing is, whatever you're going through, you don't have to do it alone. And you don't have to wait for somebody to find you. You can be the one who stands up, as I did on that night, and asks, "Is there anyone else out there who's in the same situation?"

A successful tribe looks after its members, and the good news is that you don't have to be born into one. You can always make your own.

49
Talk to a Tree

There was a song that used to make me laugh when I was little: "I talk to the trees—that's why they put me away . . ." So I don't talk to trees, but sometimes I let trees talk to me. No, of course they don't talk to me either. What I mean is that sometimes I feel a lot better when I've spent time near a tree and we've just been quiet together.

It's always worth listening to trees. They have a world of sound all their own, and the more attentively you can sit with them and open your ears and mind, the more tuned in you will become to the life, the stillness, the strength, the slow growth, and the power of sanctuary they offer.

The best moments of a stay in Crete were spent in the shade, leaning against the trunk of an ancient olive tree at the foot of the Samaria Gorge. I simply sat there, paying attention to the million-year-old flow of the rocks, the scent of the fig trees, the feather-light dance of insects swimming in the air currents, and the constant tread of thousands of walkers in the dusty path, up and down.

Then that tree got to me. After I'd spent half an hour in its company, I felt as if I'd been time-traveling. I'd detached myself from the flickering existence of the insects, even the walkers with their soft, tired flesh and brittle bones, and I had tuned in to a planetary rhythm, the infinitely slow ebb and flow that was recorded on the rock walls and in the thick, twisted sinews of the olive trees.

Time out of time is what it takes to rebalance as a human being, and time out of time is what great trees offer. It's what makes trees into teachers.

I remembered, as I got up, that people can have good ideas under the influence of trees. Hippocrates healed people under a plane tree. Isaac Newton understood the nature of gravity under an apple tree. The Buddha found enlightenment under the bodhi tree.

I'm not saying that you'll discover the secrets of the universe or attain enlightenment in the company of trees, but if you want to gain perspective, release cares, unravel problems, or simply retune your heartstrings, a tree is the place to go.

50
Consult a Life Coach

Three times in my life I've consulted a life coach, and each time I've received the encouragement and fresh thinking that allowed me to make major positive changes in my life that I wouldn't have made otherwise.

The first time I felt I needed outside help was when I seemed to have everything a woman could possibly want. I wrote a weekly column for a national newspaper and was also an executive editor, a position that came with perks such as an expense account and a nice new company car. I had a husband, two adorable little children, and a pretty house with a lovely garden in the suburbs. And somehow, with all this on my plate, I felt as if I were slipping away.

I can't remember who or what sent me to a life-coaching firm, but I found myself sitting skeptically in front of Ben, who was all of 25 years old, thinking, *How can you possibly help me make a difference in my life?* Eight weeks later, with the help of Ben's intensive, twice-weekly sessions, I had off-loaded 80 percent of my work while maintaining the same income. I'd handed over my executive role as an editor and was happily being paid for staying at home with my children and just writing my column. As each day at home passed, I felt clouds of stress lift and float away. I still use the goal-setting skills I learned from Ben, who's now a VIP in a merchant bank.

About ten years later, I found myself in a different situation. I'd been a columnist on another national newspaper for a decade, as well as a freelance writer for other papers and magazines, and was still with the children, but minus the husband. My relationship with the paper was coming to an end, but I'd been a columnist for so long that I could only think that I had to do the same song-and-dance act somewhere else. I was sitting in front of editors, swearing that I'd love to write for them, but it wasn't true.

So this time I went to see Jo Ellen. She was a coach who worked with a lot of creative clients and had a background in music and the theater. I thought she might have a different take, and I eagerly waited for her to start the same sort of "To do" lists I'd done with Ben. Instead she listened to me carefully, asked some pertinent questions, and then said, "I hear you say you've done this and achieved that and sorted out the other. Have you ever stopped?"

I was shocked, and my eyes filled with tears. Were you *allowed* to stop? Was stopping an option? As the idea penetrated my mind and I began to think if and how I could afford to take a break, I started to feel liberated, as though someone had given me the keys to my own prison. I mentally ran through my savings and decided I could afford to take the heat off myself for three months. By the time I walked back through my own front door, I'd decided to perform an experiment: For 12 weeks, I was only going to do work that absolutely excited me. And I was going to attend art school one day a week.

During those three months, I signed on for a two-year, part-time art-foundation course, while still working as a freelance journalist. I figured that if the art course proved to be too much, I could drop out. But I completed it and was offered a job as art critic on a daily paper. That was the most enjoyable and enriching job I've ever had. Two years later, I graduated with an M.A. in design and illustration, while still earning my living as a freelance journalist, because I'd discovered that when you're powered by enthusiasm and you're really focused on what you want, things fall into place. I actually earned more money in my years as a part-time art student than I had before. Of course I was working twice as hard, but I loved it.

I only went to see Jo Ellen once because she gave me one big idea and that made all the difference.

I went to Fiona two years after I finished my master's because I'd slightly run out of steam again. The thing is, life's circumstances are constantly changing, and Fiona, who was a constant source of encouragement and positive thinking, led me to the realization of a long-held fantasy.

I live and work in the city, and I've always dreamed about owning a place in the country. Fiona works by blasting you with ideas, and in one brainstorming session she made me see that there were loads of ways I could get a foothold in the country, which didn't involve buying and selling or making that scary commitment to completely pulling up my roots.

I started looking at places to lease, and by the end of the year I'd started paying rent on a furnished apartment in a village with a heart-stopping view of woods, valleys, and fields. Now I can go there and hear owls, watch buzzards, and gaze at the full moon shining on the autumn mist. I've learned a lot, and one thing—one big thing—I've learned is that I don't want to live in the country full-time. I've learned to love my dirty, overcrowded, multicultural city much more. It was worth going to Fiona to be jump-started into doing something about a dream, even if—maybe *especially* if—that dream turned out to be different from the way I'd been dreaming it.

Anyone can call him- or herself a life coach, so beware. Use referrals from friends, and compare costs—life coaches can be expensive, but if they help you create the life you want, it's worth it. Find out as much as you can about them. If you don't get a good feeling, don't go. If these coaches are any good at their job, they should help you make a real difference in your life.

51

How to Be
a River Goddess

Recently I set off for a walk along the wooded ridge on the west side of Richmond Park, where I intended to descend to cross Ham Common, and then walk through Ham village to the banks of the River Thames. Then I'd turn right and follow the towpath to Petersham, cut up River Lane, and climb to the top of Richmond Hill where I'd left my car. It should have been a good walk, but it turned into a *great* walk.

When I finally reached the riverbank at Ham, I found that I'd left something very important out of my calculations:

I'd forgotten to check the state of the tide. The Thames at Richmond is a tidal river, and at high tide the towpath often floods. So as I turned to walk toward Petersham, I found that the path was covered with a couple inches of water and that the water was rising. My path home was flooding.

I had a choice. I could turn back the way I'd come, which would be long and dreary because it was nearing sunset, the park would close, and I'd have to follow the road. *Or,* I thought, as I looked down at the dark brown water that was lapping at the toes of my shoes, *I could wade.*

I looked ahead and saw that I didn't have far to go. There was only a half mile of flooded towpath between me and Petersham, where I could turn off into the woods. The rising tide hid the edge of the riverbank, but I'd walked this path often and knew where the river lay, so there was no danger of falling in. What was the worst that could happen? I'd get my feet wet and possibly tread on something unpleasant that lay below the water.

A long, boring walk back the way I'd come . . . or a quick wade? I bent down and took off my shoes. I was wearing pantyhose, but they were just going to get wet anyway, so I turned up my pants legs and stepped into the flood tide.

At that point, I lost touch with ordinary reality and entered a new world. At first the water was just above my ankles. I could feel the stony surface of the path beneath the soles of my feet. The incoming water created a hush over everything, and there was nobody else around. Gradually, the water crept up to my knees. I had to stop and roll my pants up again. Voices floated over the river from the far bank. Suddenly I stumbled. The path had dropped away below my feet, and the cold water was now up above my knees.

I stood and worked out what had happened. I'd reached a point where a side gully left the main towpath and was carrying the floodwater in a little torrent into a field below the level of the riverbank. I realized, as I watched the tidewater gushing down this channel into the field, that I hadn't thought about changes in levels or crosscurrents.

My pants were really wet now, so there was no point in rolling them up farther, but my coat was going to get wet, so

I took that off and tied it around my shoulders. There was nobody in sight at all. I stood in a wide sheet of fast-flowing water. If I slipped and fell or got out of my depth and was swept into the river, nobody would know. But I was halfway to my exit by now, the little wood that I knew I could climb into. I was going to get wetter, but I didn't see how I could drown. Feeling with my bare feet, I advanced very carefully, and found myself back on higher ground, although I was still in the fast-flowing river up to my thighs.

Then the path dropped beneath my feet again, and this time I went in above my waist. At this point of no return, I was overcome with exhilaration. The sun was setting behind me, and a red, cloud-streaked sky was reflected in the river's shining surface. As the trees around me grew dark, the river grew light. A little fleet of ducks sailed past me, and a shimmering hush prevailed. All I could hear were river sounds: the surge and splash of my own body forging through the water, the thin sound human voices make as they cross water, the wind in the branches and the running of the water through the drowned grasses.

As I splashed nearer to the little wood, I could hear a man and woman talking. I climbed out of the water and over a bank into the trees, dripping and running with river water, my dry shoes in my hand. In front of me, in the dusky light of the wood, stood a startled young couple, dumbfounded at the sight of me, a figure appearing miraculously and silently from the depths of the river. When he found his voice, the young man said, "What are you? A river goddess or something?"

I was soaked to the bone—cold, muddy, and bedraggled—but I *felt* like a river goddess! I'd left my normal element, dry land, for an element that was much more mysterious and unpredictable. There had been a point, waist deep in the river, when I'd felt like a part of the twilight-hued world around me. I'd faced a little danger, but I'd survived. I'd taken a physical risk, but it had paid off. I'd gotten soaked, but I felt positively giggly. I'd thrown being cautious and sensible out of the window and had let myself go instead, and it felt glorious. I'd stepped out of my regulated city world and gone primitive. If that's what it feels like to be a river goddess, then, yes, for half an hour I was one.

The famous psychologist Carl Jung once said that if every man and woman could experience being primitive for five minutes a day, then he'd have no patients.

Maybe this exhilaration, this adrenaline rush, this heightened sense of being a physical creature, is behind the rising passion for extreme sports. I don't want to throw myself off a mountain, but I know that the following things are also an antidote to computer-bound, television-enslaved, car-incarcerated 21st-century life: going barefoot and feeling the world beneath the soles of your feet; walking, running, and cartwheeling on the beach; climbing hills; swimming in a river, a lake, or best of all, the sea; scrambling over trees and rocks; swinging or turning upside down; dancing; wearing as few clothes as possible; and allowing yourself to get wet in the rain.

Do any of these things sound familiar? When we did them as children, we felt fantastic. To feel as exhilarated and as connected to life as you did when you were a child, all you have to do is take off your shoes and skip out of your element!

52
When the Sea Is Your Dinner Date

I thank my friend Susie for a trick that transforms the experience of being alone. Susie and her mother and I were on a vacation in Greece, and our evening ritual was a stroll along the waterfront past all the little cafés, with their display cases of fresh fish and delicious vegetable dishes.

Every single café had an inviting little table set on the water's edge looking out over the bay, with a backdrop of sheer mountains sloping down into the clear green water. No matter which one we chose, we would take the table and turn it facing the view so that all three of us could sit and look out to sea as the sun went down. "And this," said Susie exuberantly, waving her hand over the sea, the mountains, the sunset and rocks, "is your dinner date for tonight."

Susie and her mother had to go back to work after a week, but I decided to stay on by myself. I loved the place, and I like being by myself, but anyone who travels alone knows that it's easy being on your own during the day, but eating alone in the evening feels much more solitary, especially when most of the other tables are crowded with vacationing families and couples.

But I had the sea as my dinner date. I had nobody to distract me from concentrating on the imperceptibly shifting colors of rock, sky, and water. Nobody was blocking my view of the last fishing boats coming in, the lights coming on over the water, and the fading of the mountains through soft shades of blue and lilac as the sun went down. Instead of struggling to make conversation like some of the couples around me, or dealing with tired, fractious children like some of the families,

I could focus on the red mountaintops. I could lift my glass of wine to the primal miracle of the moon rising above the rim of the sea. I took just as much care choosing my solitary viewpoint each night as I had when I was one of three. Because the sea was my dinner date, I was never bored. Because the sea was my dinner date, I never felt deprived. I felt full.

But you can't take the sea everywhere with you. And sometimes we all have to be alone . . . and it can be hard. I know a seasoned single traveler who lost weight in Athens because she couldn't muster up the courage to go into restaurants alone. Sometimes people who run such establishments are rude to single eaters and make them feel even smaller than they do already. But then, sometimes they're charming and lovely and make you feel wonderful. But not knowing which experience you're going to have adds to the fear many people have of dining alone. Some people think that other diners will think they're sad and unlovable. They should take a tip from a woman I know who assumes that if she's alone, everyone will think she's mysterious and glamorous.

But what does it matter what other people might think when your companion is the whole world? It doesn't have to be the sea. It can be a busy city sidewalk, a crowded restaurant, or a place where you can watch other people rather than a view. Or, if you're alone at home, hooray! Your dinner date needn't be the television, although that's many people's companion of choice. It can be Tolstoy, Rembrandt, a copy of *Vogue,* a book of verse, a vase of flowers, or a symphony by Tchaikovsky. Alone is never alone once you turn your attention out to the world.

53

Forever Creating

It can be a paralyzing experience trying to create something good. Instead of seeing what we do as a fluid process that can be changed, we're intimidated by the concept of perfection and comparison. Children who create freely when they're little stop in their tracks when they come up against the idea of perfection. Their flower doesn't look like a *real* flower, so they stop drawing flowers forever.

If we don't want to be permanently blocked and perpetually self-critical, we have to look at creativity differently.

I was once listening to a radio program about a village in Africa where the women are famous for decorating their houses with intricate patterns of colored mud. Their artistry is admirable, but they accept their work as a transitory thing. The sun cracks the mud and the rain washes it away, and the next season they re-create their decorated houses knowing that, however glorious their work, it won't last forever.

The villages attract visitors, photographers, and tourists, with everyone marveling at the fact that so much of the work is so ephemeral. "Isn't there a way," they ask, "that the women can fix their work in cement or translate their skills into artifacts that tourists can buy, hang on their walls, and keep forever?"

The village women think the tourists are very funny. "They have their little forevers," says one, "but we are forever creating."

When you look at creativity as a *process* instead of a *means* to produce perfection, it frees you up enormously. A friend of mine keeps a note above her desk to free her when she gets stuck writing a book. "Process not product," it says. "Privilege not pressure." The process is the point. Even great works of art are often just stills from the movie of the artist's mind. They don't leap up full formed from nowhere; they're landmarks on a long journey, and the journey is as important as the destination.

To produce, we must be able to make endless mistakes, and often the mistakes themselves are starting points for fresh approaches and new ideas. When I sit paralyzed at my desk or drawing board, thinking I should be producing something great, I have to remind myself that it really doesn't matter where I start, the point is to make for the sake of making without worrying about the finished product. That will come.

Unless we're forever creating, there won't be any forevers at all.

54

The Uses of Silence

The cure for noise is silence. Sometimes music feels like the cure for everything—the upbeat kind that sets your heart and body dancing, the solemn music that allows you to cry, the haunting music that lets you dream. But there are times to turn off the music, because silence is what you need to breathe, to uncoil, to return to a state of balance and hear the quiet call of your own heart. When life is hectic, I sometimes close a door and enter a room where there's no sound but my own breathing, and I feel profound relief.

It's very hard to find silence in a world where mechanical noise is everywhere. You can't shop, have your hair cut, check into a hotel, exercise at a gym, or even fill your car with gas without the accompaniment of someone else's sound-track. They've even put music into bookstores, the last refuge of the peaceful browser, and a railway line has just decided to put TVs above the seats, even though just about everyone I know treats a train ride as an opportunity for reading and con-templation.

But if you seek it out, there's more silence in the world than noise. You can find it if you go deep into the interior of build-ings (and people, too), and you can find it on the planet's sur-face. Recently I stood on a friend's doorstep at midnight and felt myself expand into the silence of the night. It was deep in the hill country of the north of England, and there were no cars, radios, or cell phones. All I could see was the single light of a distant farm, and all I could hear was a nearby waterfall and the wind in the trees. I could feel myself becoming calmer, taller.

Silence lets you grow. In fact I'd say that you can't grow without it. I think that unwanted sounds are like a physical assault. Something in us shrinks at the constant battering of noise, and it's only when we find a source of silence and become conscious of it that we realize how exhausting the onslaught of the sounds we haven't chosen are.

You can find silence in an empty room. There's silence in an empty church or temple. There's silence in art, in the depths of a great painting. There's silence in a vase of flowers or in the sky. And the place where there's always silence is in our own depths.

Choose a quiet place. Close your eyes to the world. Sit comfortably. Breathe gently and tune in to that inner silence . . . and you'll find that you've discovered a constant source of renewal.

55

Darkness

True darkness is a refuge and a revelation. I remember standing in a church one Christmas Eve at a candlelit service, at the moment when every light went out, and suddenly having a sense of the real power of the Christmas image of a light shining in the darkness.

Once, not so long ago, the whole world was dark. Then came electricity, and now we've become cut off from the stars. We are a neon , halogen-, floodlight-, laser-, lightbulb-dazzled generation, and most of us have never experienced true darkness at all. What we think of as darkness is no more than a deeper kind of shade. But thousands of generations before us lived in true nighttime darkness, where the light of a candle was a wonder, an image of huge power.

We use the word *darkness* as a synonym for something that's bad, but it isn't. Darkness is good. Darkness is the soil out of which we grow and to which we return. It's dark in the womb when we grow slowly, cell by cell. We seek darkness at night when we need to shut down our physical and mental body for rest and repair. It's dark in the earth where bulbs and seeds begin to unfold before spring. It's dark in the places where we dream—cinemas and theaters and our own beds. Sometimes those dreams are nightmares, but the darkness is what we need to unravel all our thoughts, both good and bad. Without darkness, as prisoners and victims of torture in their cruelly lighted cells can testify, there's no rest, only madness.

It makes me sad that children are growing into adulthood in cities all over the world without truly experiencing darkness and its revelation—a glimpse of the astonishing, mysterious universe of which our planet is a tiny part. Some people feel fear and nothingness when they gaze at the night sky and realize how infinitesimally small they are, but I find it comforting. It gives me an epic scale against which to measure my little preoccupations.

In the city, among the lights, I'm sometimes astonished by the sight of the moon over the rooftops. It's easy to forget. In the country, I hang out of my window at night, transfixed by the brilliant golden glow of Mars in the east, by the creamy dust of the Milky Way. I live in a cloudy country where a clear night sky isn't guaranteed (even if I can escape from light pollution), so I try to travel each year to a place where there's true darkness and I can see a dazzling night sky—a Mediterranean island or a North African desert. I'll never forget the magic of sailing on an Ethiopian lake at midnight, where the stars were so bright that they made tracks on the water. It's the most beautiful of paradoxes that we need to experience profound darkness in order to see the most brilliant of lights.

56
The Art of Pulling Back

Imagine that your life is a landscape and that you're a bird. Down on the ground or in a treetop you have no sense of the whole. All you can see are grass stalks, twigs and leaves, and the food that lives there.

But take off up into the sky and everything is clear. You see the grass in relation to the trees; you see the trees in relation to the ground. You see this valley and the curve that leads to the one beyond. You see the glint of water and the shape of the hunting cat.

Fly higher and you see the curve of the horizon and the nature of the approaching weather. You begin to get a sense of worlds beyond the valley, and you can catch the signals that

tell you to head south to your invisible but persistently calling destination. But you can't live up there. When you need
to eat, you must go down near the ground again and deal with
the urgency of survival, and you risk losing your sense of the
whole, your perspective, and your sense of destination.

I've learned that the art of successful living calls on the
ability to pull back and see the big picture. Some people can
operate in this way at all times, because somehow, in the
midst of chaos, they can still refer to the bird's-eye view in
their head and heart and see how everything relates. I can't do
that. I need to consciously pull back from time to time, away
from the overwhelming detail and the overload of calls for my
attention . . . and refocus.

I'm not alone in this. Spiritual disciplines have always
advocated retreats to reconnect with God or Spirit. It's common now for big companies and organizations to select those
staff members who need the overview and send them off on
seminars and meditation weekends to refocus and recharge.

People who work alone need to remember this, too. So you can't afford a week's retreat or a workshop or the services of a coach? Well, you *can* afford to take a day off, a kind of vision quest where you carry one question in your mind—*What do I do next?*—and let it simmer there while you walk, meditate, swim, or just stare into space. Even an hour where you shut the world out can make a difference.

When people who have pulled back to regain their sense of direction begin to refocus in close-up mode, they need to connect their sense of wider vision with the demands of the everyday world. They must have a strategy that connects the bird's-eye view with the demanding short-term world of the grass stalks.

I find that it helps to answer the question: *What can I do in the next 20 minutes that will take me in the direction I want to go?* It could be writing a letter, making a phone call, paying off a debt, joining a weight-loss support group, starting a file for a project, or delegating a project to somebody else. But it mustn't be big. It should be writing an outline for a novel, not writing the whole book. Thinking too big on the ground only leads to paralysis.

These are the guidelines: Think very big. Think very small. Learn to go back and forth easily between different lengths of focus. Think horizons and weather systems. Think grass stalks and twigs. If you stay in the clouds, you won't eat. If you stay on the ground, you might get eaten. If you dream too much, you'll get lost in inertia because nothing you try will measure up to your dream. If you're run off your feet with details and other people's demands, you're in danger of losing your inner map, your bigger picture.

If and when you do follow these guidelines, you might become one of those rare people whose bigger dreams drive and inspire others.

57

Be Truly Democratic

I interviewed a king once. His name was King Simeon of Bulgaria, and he had the best manners of anyone I've ever met. At the time I met him, he was in his 50s and had been living in exile from his country since the age of 9—and all that time he'd led a double life.

He'd created a working life for himself as a businessman, he'd brought up five children to be self-supporting and have careers of their own, and he'd also held a torch for the freeing of Bulgaria from years of Communism, whether or not his country ever wanted him back. He may have lived most of his life as an exile in Spain but, unlike most ex-kings who have been booted out of their countries, he had never abdicated.

King Simeon had every reason to nurture a rather grand idea of himself. When he was born in 1937, there was a 150-gun salute; a three-day national holiday; amnesty was given for thousands of political prisoners; and there was a mass pilgrimage to the palace of peasants bearing flowers, fruit, and even little pigs.

At 11 days old, the little crown prince entered his country's army as 2nd Lieutenant of the 6th Infantry Regiment, Commander of the 19th Infantry Regiment, and Commander of the 3rd Cavalry Regiment. A photograph shows the infant prince in full military uniform surrounded by a loyal armed guard. But when his father, King Boris of Bulgaria, died suddenly, the six-year-old prince's life became, in his own words, "rather gruesome," and led him, after some homeless years, to live in Spain.

There are different ways of living out the uprooted life of an exiled king. One of them involves the erasing of memory and the denial of the past. Another involves a rootless playboy existence, avoiding all responsibilities and drawing on the social credit of a title. King Simeon's way was the democratic way, which is to say that he behaved with perfect courtesy to everyone and assumed responsibility but no privilege.

When I met him, he addressed me as "ma'am" and the photographer as "sir." He had no entourage, and he listened to us with rapt attention, answered all my questions thoughtfully and gravely, and obeyed the photographer's instructions patiently. I've interviewed movie stars, opera singers, politicians, presidents, artists, writers, tycoons, and models, all of whom were enjoying their moment of fame and consequence—and not one of them had manners that matched the modest consideration and courtesy of King Simeon of Bulgaria.

So it was no surprise to me that when Bulgaria finally shook off Communism and re-created itself as a democracy, King Simeon was invited back, by popular demand, to be the first president. The last I heard, the honeymoon between exiled king and country was over, and people were as disillusioned by him as they are by any politician, but that doesn't negate the point I'm trying to make here. All around me, every day, I hear people being rude and abusive to each other. They may win a point with sheer aggression, but they make the world a more unpleasant and dangerous place.

Who do they think they are . . . royalty? If I'm tempted to be rude, I remember King Simeon, because he taught me that being truly democratic means that you treat everyone as if they were royalty, even if you are in fact a real, live king.

58
Life Is a Work in Progress

I can't bear it when people say they're failures. Few things upset me more than seeing someone, especially somebody young, crumpled in a miserable heap because they think that they've failed. If that's you, stop it. Peel the label off and throw it away. Right now. Because you're not a failure; you're a work in progress. You've just hit a bump in the road where you feel like you're not progressing.

Maybe I was just born this way, but even on the most stomach-turning drops on the roller coaster of life, it never occurs to me to think of myself as a failure. So something didn't work out. Maybe it was a big thing like a job or a marriage and I'm brokenhearted, but that still doesn't make me a failure. It makes me a person whose marriage broke up or who's reached a place that may require some creative résumé writing. The word *failure* is like a big black mark, but there are no black marks in life. Everything is fluid. Everything changes. Even the darkest moments are temporary stages in a long, unfolding journey that really only ends in death. And maybe not even then.

When I was a child, I figured out that life was full of surprises, and you could never know the sum of it until it was over—and even then it was open to interpretation, otherwise why would people keep rewriting biographies and history books? I was really pleased to find out that someone (Solon the Athenian lawgiver, in fact) said back in the fifth-century B.C.: "Call no man happy till he is dead." Call no man or woman a failure either.

If I reject the idea of failure, it's because of its finality. People who think of themselves as failures are accepting self-imposed defeat, and it paralyzes them. But life is movement, and the important thing is to keep moving, try another angle, take another shot. That way you learn that there's a world of difference between reaching a dead end and setting up home in it. Above all, never, ever send out change-of-address cards.

59

Be Your Own Resource

We all know more than we think we do. We've all done things that worked, things that excited us, things that gave us glimpses of ourselves as we'd like to be, and showed us life as we'd like to experience it. And then we forget it all.

This is a great mystery. Why is it so easy to forget even the good things, the moments of understanding and insight, the times when the whole pattern becomes clear? I think it's because life is so fast moving, so fragmented, and so complex. It's not just our own story that we're living, it's the related stories of millions of other people, all with their own states of confusion.

The air is full of static. Newspapers, television, radio, the Internet, cell phones, e-mails, books, the cinema, music,

art, theater, fashion, shopping, advertising, politics, bureau-
cracy, other people's demands on us at work, families, and so
forth all clamor for our attention before we've even spent five
minutes paying attention to the one person who's most important to us: ourselves. There's no time to think, no space to feel.

If you live life unconsciously, allowing your time and
movements to be driven by external forces, then you're in danger of leaving the ground altogether, of becoming a tumble-
weed blowing across the desert. The look I see on many people's faces, especially traveling to work in the city, is one of
exhausted bewilderment: *How did I get here? How do I get out?*
It doesn't matter how old you are; if anything, it's the younger
people—those in their 20s and 30s—who complain that
they're shattered.

If this is you, nobody's going to stop the merry-go-round
but you. It's not about changing your life all at once. It's
about finding a moment of authenticity and self-truth. These
moments are the places you can stand on to change the world.
Your starting place is a moment of quiet reflection (although

you can do this with friends) and something to write with. Once the momentum is going, this is a pleasurable, even inspiring, exercise. I remember doing it with Ben, my first life coach, and he always said it was his favorite part of the job.

Think back to those moments when you felt fully yourself, completely alive. Were you five years old? Fifteen? Thirty? Where were you? What were you doing? Who were you with? Was it something you did once or something that's now integrated into your life? Was it a moment of play or part of your working life? Would you love to do it again? How did you feel afterward? Was there a hangover of some kind, or were you inspired and energized?

And there's another kind of list, a list of the times when you were in doubt or difficulty and survived. What got you out of it? Was it help from friends, taking control yourself, learning new skills, getting medical assistance, following a spiritual practice, taking a stand, enrolling in a workshop, reading a book, seeing a therapist, building on a chance encounter with a stranger, or simply taking time out   in the form of a sabbatical, a vacation, or a leave of absence? Did you take notes or keep a diary? If so, dig them out.

I don't know what any of these answers will be for you. But when you've gathered all this material (and it may take some time), you will. And you'll have your resource book. Put it together. Stick a label on it. Present it to yourself as formally and as attractively as you like: *"Everything I've Ever Done That Worked. By Me."*

60
The Refugee's Guide to Being Human

Sometimes people lose everything. The crisis that comes into their lives isn't one of the heart, the ego, or the bank balance. They haven't lost a job, a lover, or even a limb. Their view of their future hasn't simply vanished as a castle in the air quivers and melts in the mind; it has crumbled into real dust before their physical eyes. A familiar wall hides a sniper. A beloved home explodes in flames. The men who support you are killed or have vanished. The women you love and honor are raped. The children starve. The country lies in ruins. What, in these extremes of human experience, works?

One hot May day in 1999, I walked on a Macedonian hillside among people who were barely living a human existence. The hillside had been bulldozed bare of all vegetation, even grass. The green hills of the Balkans were all around, but wire fences marked out blinding acres of rough stones. I was in Cigrane, the latest refugee camp created in Macedonia for the thousands of refugees fleeing across the borders from Kosovo. It was for Albanian Kosovars who had abandoned their homes to Serbian militia and who had spent days and weeks trekking through the mountains to a place of safety.

Cigrane wasn't a place where anyone wanted to be. It was so new and raw that tents were still being erected, and families were sleeping out on uncushioned stones on the bare mountainside. Outside the camp gates waited red buses crammed with exhausted people who had lined up to walk across the Macedonian border. I'd seen the buses earlier waiting at the border post and the shocked, drained, and exhausted faces of the people in them were like no human faces I'd ever seen before. They were the faces of people who had surrendered, the unfocused, burnt-out visages of people at the edge of endurance. When I saw them, I thought I knew what the Jews looked like on the trains that took them to the concentration camps.

Five thousand people a day were coming into Cigrane. While the newest group of refugees waited passively in the buses, inside the gates I walked about and talked to the people who had already been there a night. A system was beginning to establish itself: Where tents had been erected and blankets distributed, the human urge to create a home was asserting itself.

People had no more than the clothes they'd been wearing when they fled the Serbs. To have clean clothes, they had to lie naked under their blankets while their clothes dried on the ropes of their tent. Mothers with babies lined up in the hot May sun for the daily ration of three disposable diapers a day. Further down the hillside, a truck unloaded the sole food allowance of one roll of bread a day. There was another line at a table set up by the Red Cross to register people looking for lost relatives.

Everywhere I walked I could feel a palpable atmosphere of bewilderment, fatigue, and frustration. These were the surface emotions stirred up by the chaos of the camp. Beneath the minute-by-minute anxiety of trying to function in this raw, hostile environment, each individual was holding deeper feelings of loss, grief, and a terrible fear of what the future might bring.

And yet in the most difficult circumstances, the human spirit irresistibly asserts itself. Children were playing and laughing by the water pipes. Little twig brooms already stood outside the doors of the tents as a witness to the effort to create order out of overwhelming disorder.

I'll never forget standing on the most exposed area of the camp, a white slope of sharp stones scattered with the belongings of the small groups of people who'd spent the night on the open mountainside. I was talking to a weary middle-aged couple about their sleepless night when a striking little group came straggling up the hillside toward us. Like Mother Courage, Begishe, a 32-year-old woman, grubby but spirited, was leading her ragtag band of five children up the hill. They were dusty-faced, weary, their arms full of bags and blankets and babies. They'd been sleeping under the stars and on the stones of Cigrane for five days. Before that, Begishe had led them through the mountains from village to village, ever since the Serbian militia had attacked their village and driven them up into makeshift shelters in the forest. Their father was in Germany, but the dusty little family radiated a tough spirit of survival and resilience.

As they stood talking to the older couple, I expressed my inadequate sympathy for their situation, and it was my awkward words of kindness rather than their hardship that brought tears to their eyes. I wanted to know what it was that gave them the spirit and courage to keep going in these extreme and chaotic circumstances. It was the older woman who told me, "We do everything together. We give each other moral support. We are very human to each other."

It was a very striking and humbling lesson. When every-thing intangible has gone—status, worldly identity, optimism for the future, ambition—people can still be human to each other. When everything tangible has gone—home, land, fam-ily, farm animals, clothes, and possessions—people can still be human to each other. Being human is all they have left.

What did this woman mean, homeless on her open moun-tainside, by being human? After all, the gunmen who had driven these people out of their homes and country were being human, too. I've thought often about this, and I think that being human means being vulnerable and open. It means being in sympathy with other people and knowing that you're not different from them. It means being part of one organism, not safe or separate. It means abandoning roles, expecta-tions, judgments, and opposition. It means losing the need to control other people. It means being responsive to your envi-ronment and not shut off from it, let alone seized by the need to exploit and destroy it. It means reaching out rather than shutting off. It certainly *doesn't* mean discriminating, oppressing, excluding, and even killing.

Good fortune and bad fortune can both encourage a sense of humanity. Good fortune does it by making us relaxed, trusting, and unafraid; bad fortune by making us recognize our irreducible human nature and our interdependency with others. But good fortune carries the danger of complacency and detachment from other people's experiences. The enclaves of the rich aren't famous for their humanity, however many checks the rich may sign for the poor. It's ironic that the great qualities of openness, generosity, and kindness often only surface in extreme circumstances—the London Blitz, September 11 in America. In circumstances of overwhelming threat, when everything familiar has gone, being human is all that works.

Like everything else in this book, when the circumstances change, the lesson is in danger of being lost. I once heard Ram Dass say that the challenge of life is to keep your heart open in hell. They were striking words, but when I remember those Kosovars in the stones and dust, I wonder if it isn't easier to keep your heart open in hell when your heart is all that's left. The challenge is to stay human when the complexity of daily life returns, along with the suffocation of possessions and the seeking and maintaining of status.

That's one reason why I wrote this book. Time and again, in difficult circumstances, I've found something that worked, only to forget it again when the difficulty passed.

I know one truth: As sure as the sun rises, life will get difficult again, which is why I hope that by writing these things down I'll remember them for myself and why I pass them on to you . . . in the sincere hope that they'll help in the magnificent but sometimes overwhelming business of *being human*.

Acknowledgments

This is both my acknowledgment of my debt of gratitude, and my dedication of this book to those who have helped and accompanied me.

This little book represents the distillation of years of my own efforts to get a grip on both happiness and the meaning of life. Luckily for me, there was always good company along the way. Some people have been there for the long haul, others simply shared a part of the journey. Some just said or did the thing that made all the difference at the time. Some were fellow students, some valued teachers, and of course, it's quite possible to be both at once.

The following people have given me friendship, support, lessons, common sense, encouragement, direction, humor, wisdom, and invaluable companionship: Thank you very much indeed to Marianna Alexander; Gay Baynes; Leonard Bernstein; David Braybrook; Ben Cannon; Anne Dickson; Frances d'Souza; Jo Ellen Grzyb; Gloria Karpinski; Malcolm and Jane Lazarus; Gavin Maughling; Sheila Morley; Caroline Mustill; Carole Radford; Caroline Reynolds; Jenny Ridgewell; Veronica Roberts; Deidre, Rick, and Susie Sanders; and Mike Ward.

In direct connection with this book, I especially want to thank Mick Brown, Jilly Cooper, and Max Hastings for their hugely appreciated encouragement; and the team at Hay House—Jo Lal, Megan Slyfield, and most particularly Michelle Pilley—for their responsiveness, care, and professionalism.

And of course I want to thank my immediate family—my parents for their wisdom and example, and my two daughters, Harriet and Rachel—for their energy and their continual and invaluable reminder that you can be happy, wise, and optimistic without ever taking any courses at all.

Reading and Resource List

Books are an ever-present source of inspiration, so here is a short list of titles that I've found helpful and friendly. If I were to list everything that has inspired, stimulated, comforted, and enriched me over the course of a lifetime, it would take *another* whole book.

Self-help books perform a very useful function, but the more challenging the books and the more deeply you read, the more you'll get out of your life. Explore it all—poetry, philosophy, fiction, science, biography, travel, and memoir. Here are some of my recommendations in no particular order:

An Autobiography by M. K. Gandhi (1929; Penguin, 1982) or *The Golden String* by Bede Griffiths (Fount, 1979).

These books will give you an idea of how a person's life can be inspired and influenced by their reading.

Performance: Revealing the Orpheus Within by Anthony Rooley (Element Books, 1984). A musician's look at the relationship between preparation and inspiration.

The Meditator's Handbook by David Fontana (HarperCollins, 1992). A clear and comprehensive account of different forms of meditation with plenty of practical exercises.

The Miracle of Mindfulness by Thich Nhat Hanh (Rider, 1991). A small classic of Buddhist meditation, written so clearly that a child could understand it.

A Woman in Your Own Right by Anne Dickson (Quartet, 1982). The standard work on assertiveness training.

Spiritual Fitness by Caroline Reynolds (HarperCollins, 2001). A specific course of exercises you can follow to deepen your experience of life.

Sabbath Rest by Wayne Muller (Lion, 2000). A heartfelt case for restoring rest and rhythm into stressed-out modern lives.

The Mozart Effect by Don Campbell (Hodder & Stoughton, 2002). A well-argued and densely illustrated case for the crucial role of music in our life and health.

A Compendium of Flower Essences by Clare G. Harvey, Peter Tadd, and Don Dennis, published in 2002 by International Flower Essence Repertoire (IFER) at The Living Tree, Milland, near Liphook, Hampshire, GU30 7JS; tel: 011-44-1428 741572. An eye-opener for anyone who thinks that the only flower remedies are the Bach essences. IFER sells most of these essences from their shop in Hampshire, and it's well worth a visit. I defy anyone to go there and walk out without buying. They're very knowledgeable and also run weekend courses. The Australian Bush Flower Essences are quite widely available from branches of Neal's Yard or Fresh & Wild.

I also recommend *Australian Bush Flower Essences* by Ian White (Findhorn Press, 1993) and *Australian Bush Flower Healing* by Ian White (Bantam, 1999).

The definitive layperson's guide to cognitive behavior therapy is *Feeling Good* by David D. Burns, M.D. (Avon Health, 1999).

Also recommended is *The Feeling Good Handbook* by David D. Burns, M.D. (Plume, 2000).

Be Your Own Life Coach by Fiona Harrold (Hodder Mobius, 2001). A brisk and practical introduction to life coaching from one of the UK's most high-profile and experienced coaches.

Crystal Power, Crystal Healing by Michael Gienger (Cassell and Co, 1998). There are plenty of books about crystals and many of them, frankly, are more poetry and fairy tale than science, but this has very good photographs and some actual geological information along with the healing associations of each stone.

The Artist's Way by Julia Cameron (Tarcher/Putnam, 1998). This is a classic of self-help and creativity for anyone and everyone who doubts their ability to be creative. It's well written, practical, very encouraging, and the focus for a number of support groups.

Finding Your Own North Star by Martha Beck (Piatkus, 2001). This is where I found the Beauty Way, but Martha Beck has plenty of good techniques to help you shut out the noise and find your own way.

Where Two Worlds Touch and *Barefoot on Holy Ground,* both by Gloria Karpinski (Ballantine, 1990 and 2001). Gloria sees life as a spiritual journey and brings a lifetime of practice to her understanding of how we can stay in touch with the spirit in the midst of busy lives.

Molecules of Emotion by Candace B. Pert (Prentice Hall, 1997). Here comes the science. . . . Psychoneuroimmunologist Candace Pert explains, in terms that even I can understand, how emotions are chemistry and vice versa. She also gives practical suggestions for helping our body to be its own healer and tran-quillizer.

and for information on . . .

. . . Emotional Freedom Technique—there are few books but many Websites. Plug in "emotional freedom technique" into **www.Google.com** and you will find plenty of leads. And the Website **www.meridiantherapies.org** has a quick two-minute stress-relief technique you can follow on the screen.

Romas Foord

About the Author

Lesley Garner has been taking notes all her life. Her thoughts and observations have been published as magazine features, profiles, and newspaper columns for publications such as the *London Daily Telegraph, Daily Mail,* and *Evening Standard* in the UK. She has been an art critic, a book and film reviewer, and when she's not writing, she loves to get out and sing great choral music. She has traveled widely, has lived in Ethiopia and Afghanistan, and currently lives in London.

Notes

Notes

Notes

Notes

Sign up via the Hay House USA Website to receive the
Hay House online newsletter and stay informed about what's
going on with your favorite authors. You'll receive bimonthly
announcements about: Discounts and Offers, Special Events,
Product Highlights, Free Excerpts, Giveaways, and more!
www.hayhouse.com

We hope you enjoyed this Hay House book. If you'd like to receive a free catalog featuring additional Hay House books and products, or if you'd like information about the Hay Foundation, please contact:

Hay House, Inc., P.O. Box 5100, Carlsbad, CA 92018-5100

(760) 431-7695 or **(800) 654-5126**
(760) 431-6948 (fax) or **(800) 650-5115 (fax)**
www.hayhouse.com

Published and distributed in Australia by: Hay House Australia Pty. Ltd. • 18/36 Ralph St. • Alexandria NSW 2015 • *Phone:* 612-9669-4299 • *Fax:* 612-9669-4144 • www.hayhouse.com.au

Published and distributed in the United Kingdom by:
Hay House UK, Ltd. • Unit 62, Canalot Studios • 222 Kensal Rd., London W10 5BN • *Phone:* 44-20-8962-1230 • *Fax:* 44-20-8962-1239
www.hayhouse.co.uk

Published and distributed in the Republic of South Africa by:
Hay House SA (Pty), Ltd., P.O. Box 990, Witkoppen 2068
Phone/Fax: 2711-7012233 • orders@psdprom.co.za

Distributed in Canada by: Raincoast • 9050 Shaughnessy St., Vancouver, B.C. V6P 6E5 • *Phone:* (604) 323-7100 • *Fax:* (604) 323-2600